C000263615

Isaac Watts

His Life and Thought

All of us have benefited from the ministry of the hymn writer, Isaac Watts His courage to promote a Biblical theology of hymnody united with his competency to produce hymns of musical excellence while singable for congregations, marked by excellence in style and Biblical faithfulness have provided a legacy which finds its fulfillment in the worship of the triune God of glory. But now, in this volume, Graham Beynon, allows us to meet Isaac Watts, himself, his redeemed life, saturated with the grace of God and absorbed with the glory of God. It will be hard to stop turning the pages.

Harry L. Reeder
Pastor of Preaching and Leadership, Briarwood Presbyterian Church
Birmingham, Alabama

In this thoroughly enjoyable and stimulating book, Graham Beynon does an excellent job of showing just how relevant Watts and his thought are for today. We get to see how his beautiful hymnody flowed out of deep theological and pastoral convictions, and the result is both challenging and stirring.

Michael Reeves
Theologian-at-Large, Wales Evangelical School of Theology
Bridgend, Wales

I can think of few men who have impacted my life and thought more than Isaac Watts. He is a model pastor, thinker and poet. In this engaging and thorough book, Graham Beynon presents a full and fascinating picture of Watts' legacy, from his hymns to his pastoral work to his logic. In an age of celebrity pastors, heavy on flash and low on substance, Watts presents an alternate vision: a rigorous mind at work for the glory of God and the good of the church.

Mike Cosper
Pastor of Worship and Arts, Sojourn Community Church
Louisville, Kentucky

Isaac Watts

His Life and Thought

G RAHAM B EYNON

CHRISTIAN
FOCUS

Unless otherwise indicated Scripture quotations are taken from the *The Holy Bible, New International Version®*, NIV® Copyright © 1973, 1978, 1984, 2011 by Biblica, Inc.™ Used by permission. All rights reserved worldwide.

Scripture quotations marked KJV are taken from The King James Version. All rights reserved.

Graham Beynon is minister of Grace Church, Cambridge. He is also the course director for 'TEAM' (Training for East Anglia Ministry). His PhD research was on the theology of Isaac Watts. He is married to Charis and they have three children.

Copyright © Graham Beynon 2013

paperback ISBN 978-1-78191-265-2
epub ISBN 978-1-78191-280-5
Mobi ISBN 978-1-78191-281-2

10 9 8 7 6 5 4 3 2 1

Published in 2013
by
Christian Focus Publications Ltd,
Geanies House, Fearn,
Ross-shire, IV20 1TW, Scotland.
www.christianfocus.com

Cover design
by
Daniel van Straaten

Printed by
Bell and Bain, Glasgow

All rights reserved. No part of this publication may be reproduced, stored in a retrieval system, or transmitted, in any form, by any means, electronic, mechanical, photocopying, recording or otherwise without the prior permission of the publisher or a licence permitting restricted copying. In the U.K. such licences are issued by the Copyright Licensing Agency, Saffron House, 6-10 Kirby Street, London, EC1 8TS. www.cla.co.uk

CONTENTS

DEDICATION

To Julian and Andy, with whom I have had the pleasure and privilege to work. I thank God for such mentors, colleagues and friends in ministry.

PREFACE

I've often read Christian biographies while on holiday—usually books which I've picked up second-hand which have then sat on my shelf until another holiday rolls around. So, some years ago I sat on a campsite in France reading a biography of Isaac Watts. I had bought it knowing that he was a hymn writer and that I knew nothing else about him. Little did I know that what I read would lead on to reading more about Watts, then some of his own works, and then eventually to doing a Ph.D.!

I always wanted what I discovered about Watts to be available to a wider audience, and that is what's resulted in this book. This book, however, is not simply an easier read of my Ph.D. thesis. It is much wider in scope and tries to give an overview of his whole life. I have also written assuming no knowledge of Watts or his times to make this accessible to anyone who is interested. What I have aimed at is both a biography of his life and an insight into his thought. My hope is that we will both gain a greater understanding and respect for Watts himself and also learn lessons for Christian life today.

I have quoted extensively from Watts. I should point out that I have updated the spelling, punctuation and some of the words used for the sake of clarity. For example, a 'pathetic' sermon in the eighteenth century was a 'heartfelt' sermon, not a rubbish one! Rather than explain changes in language, I've simply replaced words with their modern equivalent where necessary. I have given references to both Watts' works and other biographies and sources. The source for Watts' writings I have used is the first edition of his collected works. These are not available to purchase today, but some are available online.[1]

Thanks is due to a number of people: to Willie MacKenzie, of Christian Focus, for his enthusiasm about a book on Isaac Watts; to Rebecca Rine for her careful editing and improving on my style; and to those who read a draft of this book and made helpful comments: Joanna Scoones, Tim Grant and especially Robert Strivens.

---

1   Isaac Watts, *The Works of the Late Reverend and Learned Isaac Watts, D.D. published by himself, and now collected into six volumes. Revised and corrected by D. Jennings, D.D. and the late P. Doddridge, D.D.* (London: T. and T. Longman, and J. Buckland; J. Oswald; J. Waugh; and J. Ward, 1753).

1
FORMATIVE TIMES

An imprisoned father and a lonely mum

A young mum sat on a step outside a jail with an infant clinging on to her. Her husband was inside the jail and she was now caring for their first child by herself. So began the early life of Isaac Watts. The place was Southampton on the south coast of England. The date was 1674. Isaac Watts' dad – who confusingly was also called Isaac – was not in jail for anything that we would have considered illegal, but because of the religious situation in England at the time. Back in 1660 there had been a re-establishment of the monarchy in England after the commonwealth under Oliver Cromwell. One of the results of this change of government was a change in the church.

The Church of England was the official church of the country and everyone was supposed to join in – it was called 'conforming'. If you didn't attend the established church, you were called a 'nonconformist'. In Anglican churches there was a set liturgy of what would be said and done. Nonconformists, though, wanted to organize the content of their services themselves, either out of principle, or because they didn't think the Anglican liturgy was what it should be.

A law was passed in 1662 enforcing the use of the official Anglican liturgy. This resulted in around two thousand ministers choosing to leave the Church of England

and becoming 'nonconformists'. New churches sprang up all over the country. Often congregations followed their minister out of the Anglican Church. They met in barns, fields or private houses. These were now 'illegal' congregations.

Such a church started in Southampton, led by Nathaniel Robinson. He had been the Rector of All Saints Church, but now led a group of nonconformists who met near the Bar Gate in the centre of the city. This church eventually became known as 'Above Bar Congregational Church'.

Nonconformists were regarded as a threat to the Government and a potential cause of civil unrest. So, to keep everyone in line, a series of laws against them was passed. If you failed to attend an Anglican service, you could be fined for each occasion. If you were rebellious enough to actually organize a non-conformist church yourself and run a meeting, then you might be fined or imprisoned. This is why Isaac Watts senior was in jail. He had become one of the leaders (a deacon) at the Above Bar Congregational Church. And for doing so, he was imprisoned. He was later released, but occasional further imprisonments followed.

These hard times tested what one really believed. The prospect of punishment meant that people only went to a nonconformist church out of real conviction. They were convinced that the Anglican Church was still far too Roman Catholic in many of its practices and especially in the liturgy used in the services. Many also believed that they should have the right to organize their own church meetings rather than having to stick to a set liturgy.

This was the time that many famous nonconformist ministers wrote a lot of their works, because they were so often denied the role of pastor. John Bunyan, for example, wrote his famous *The Pilgrim's Progress* while in Bedford prison. John Owen was also recognized as one of the leaders of this movement. He was a minister in London, and Isaac Watts would eventually become one of his successors.

It's worthwhile for those of us who have the freedom to worship as we want today to reflect: are we grateful for such freedom? And do we have convictions about how we should worship which would survive the pressure of persecution?

The influence of godly parents

Young Isaac, then, was brought up in a religious home and a nonconformist church, both of which were to have profound effects on his own life. He heard the gospel at an early age, was taught about living the Christian life, and saw what it was to suffer for your convictions.

Isaac was the eldest of eight children, although, sadly, his youngest two sisters both died in their first years of life. All of the children's names are written inside a large family Bible which is now kept in the University Library in Southampton. We can assume that Isaac's father read from that very Bible in their home, teaching the children the good news about Jesus. The children were also taught the basics of the faith by catechisms – a series of questions and answers which were memorized. However, persecution soon interrupted their family life and cast its shadow again. Isaac wrote in a notebook about significant events in his life.[1] One of the early entries reads like this:

> 1683: My father persecuted and imprisoned for non-conformity six months. After that forced to leave his family and live privately in London for two years.

Isaac was now nine years old, and his father's absence would have made life difficult for this young family. We have a letter from Isaac Watts senior to his children during this time. This gives us a feel for both his concerns and his priorities for them. This is how he begins:

> My dear children,
>
> Though it has pleased the only wise God to suffer the malice of ungodly men, the enemies of Jesus Christ (and my enemies for his sake), to break out so far against me, as to remove me from you in my personal habitation, thereby

---

1   This is available to read in Paxton Hood, *Isaac Watts: His Life and Hymns* (Belfast: Ambassador, 2001).

at once bereaving me of that comfort, which I might have hoped for in the enjoyment of my family in peace, and you of that education, which my love as a father and duty as a parent required me to give; yet such are the longings of my soul for your good and prosperity, especially in spiritual concernments, that I remember you always with myself in my daily prayers addressed to the throne of grace.

It's a long sentence – but it is full of tender concern for his children, awareness of his responsibilities to them and confidence in God's sovereign rule. He later gives some specific instruction. First, about the Bible:

I charge you frequently to read the holy scriptures; and that not as a task or burden laid on you, but get your hearts to delight in them. There are the only pleasant histories which are certainly true, and greatly profitable; there are abundance of precious promises made to sinners, such as you are by nature; there are sweet invitations and counsels of God and Christ, to come in and lay hold of them; there are the choice heavenly sayings and sermons of the Son of God, the blessed prophets and apostles...The sum of all the counsel I can give you, necessary for the regulating of your behaviour towards God and man, in every station, place and condition of your lives, is contained in that blessed word of God.

So, the authority of the Bible is clear, and the sufficiency of the Bible is clear, but so is the precious nature of the Bible. It's not only something to be known and obeyed but something to be treasured and rejoiced in.

Secondly, their father said they should reflect on their sinfulness and God's salvation:

Consider seriously and often the sinful and miserable estate you are in by nature, and that you are liable to eternal wrath thereupon; also think upon the way of fallen man's recovery by grace, according to the foundational principles of the Christian religion, which you have learned in your catechism; and beg of God by prayer to give you understanding in them, and faith to believe in Jesus Christ, and a heart willing to yield obedience to his gospel commands in all things.

Notice the expectation to remind yourself of these foundational truths 'seriously and often'. Notice also the need to pray that God would give us understanding and obedience. Watts' father points here to the essential truth that we can know the gospel in theory but our hearts can remain hard.

Third, he speaks about growth in knowledge of God:

> Learn to know God according to the discoveries he has made of himself in and by his word, in all his glorious attributes and infinite perfections; especially learn to know him in and through the Lord Jesus Christ, and to be acquainted with this blessed redeemer of God's elect.

Then he moves to the duty to worship God:

> Remember that God is your Creator, from whom you received life and being; and as such you are bound to worship him; much more when you consider that he is your Benefactor, from the fountain of whose goodness all your mercies come…

> Know this, that as you must worship God, so it must be in his own ways, with true worship and in a right manner; that is according to the rules of the gospel, and not according to the inventions or traditions of men.

This last point is, of course, the reason for his previous imprisonment and now his absence. Isaac Watts senior considered the Anglican Church of the day to have many 'inventions or traditions of men' which carried over from the Roman Catholic Church. He gives specific warning against these 'popish doctrines'.

Lastly, he wisely cautions his children against being angry with God because of the persecution they are suffering:

> Do not entertain any hard thoughts of God, or of his ways, because his people are persecuted for them. For Jesus Christ himself was persecuted to death by wicked men, for preaching the gospel and doing good, and the holy apostles and prophets were cruelly used for serving God in his own way.

He goes on to speak of contentment in suffering and thanksgiving for every mercy they enjoy.

The letter ends with some lovely words about the children's mother and how they should act:

> Consider, she is left alone to bear all the burden of bringing you up; and is, as it were, a widow. Her time is filled up with many cares, and therefore do not grieve her by any rebellious or disobedient ways, but be willing to learn of her and be ruled by her, that she may have some comfort in seeing your obedient carriage; and that it will rejoice me to hear it.

> These things I charge and command you with the authority and love of a father. Now commending you to God, and what I have written to his blessing upon your hearts, through Jesus Christ, with my dear love to your mother ...[2]

Assuming this letter is a taste of Isaac Watts' childhood, we can see the wonderful influence of godly parents. It is expressed in the language of the day, but there is great Biblical concern and direction, and great love and warmth. That's an excellent model for parents to follow.

Formative education

Isaac was a bright boy. He started to learn Latin from his father at age four, Greek at nine, French at ten and Hebrew at thirteen. While that sounds amazing to us, it wasn't so unusual back then, but he was still obviously very clever. He went to school when he was six to what was simply called the 'Free School' in Southampton (now King Edward VI Grammar School). Here he was instructed by John Pinhorne, a local Anglican minister. Isaac took to his headmaster, and from a poem he later dedicated to him we can see that he clearly felt very indebted for his education. The poem ends:

> Forgive Rev. Sir, the vain attempt, and
> kindly accept this poetical fragment,

---

2   David G. Fountain, *Isaac Watts Remembered* (Harpenden: Gospel Standard Baptist Trust, 1974), pp. 17-19.

though rude and unpolished, as an
expression of that gratitude which has
been so long due to your merit.[3]

One particular influence we should note is that Pinhorne helped direct the young Isaac's poetic interest. He introduced him to the work of a Polish poet, Casimire, many of whose works Watts would later translate into English (Casimire wrote in Latin, so, no, Isaac hadn't learnt Polish as well!). Pinhorne also impressed on Watts the need for poetry to be used in service to God, which is certainly what Watts eventually did in his hymns.

Watts showed not only early interest but also skill in poetry. When he was six, he wrote a poem called an 'acrostic', where each line begins with the successive letter of his name. Here it is:

I am a vile polluted lump of earth,
So I've continued ever since my birth;
Although Jehovah grace does daily give me,
As sure this monster Satan will deceive me,
Come, therefore, Lord, from Satan's claws relieve me.

Wash me in thy blood, O Christ,
And grace divine impart,
Then search and try the corners of my heart,
That I in all things may be fit to do
Service to thee, and sing thy praises too.[4]

The fact that this was written by a six-year-old shows two things: he's a budding poet and he knows his theology!

The period of persecution against nonconformists came to an end in 1688 with what was called 'The Glorious Revolution'. Opposition had grown against King James because of his Catholic leanings, and, more importantly, his Catholic son who would succeed him. He was forced to flee the country, and his sister Mary took the throne with her husband William of Orange, from Holland, both of whom

---

3   Thomas D.D. Gibbons, *Memoirs of Isaac Watts* (London, 1780), p. 19.
4   Fountain, *Watts*, p. 14.

were invited because of their Protestant convictions. Before long an act of 'toleration', which allowed nonconformists to meet freely, was passed. The fines and imprisonments were over. Watts' local church was free to meet and began leasing a 'meeting house' for Sunday worship.

It was around this time that Watts speaks of coming to faith himself. We know that he had known about the gospel from an early age because of the teaching from his parents; and his poem above clearly showed he knew the doctrines of sin and atonement. In fact, that poem shows clear signs of conviction of sin and trust in Christ. But for children brought up in a Christian family, ownership of such beliefs usually increases with time. So, when Watts was fourteen he wrote in his notebook:

> Fell under considerable convictions of sin, 1688.
> And was taught to trust in Christ I hope, 1689.

This, of course, is what every parent hopes and prays for: not just knowledge of the gospel but conviction of sin and trust in Jesus for salvation.

New ways of thinking

Isaac finished school two years later at sixteen. Now he had to decide about further education, and here his young convictions came into play. There were still disadvantages to being a nonconformist; they were tolerated but not yet made equal. Nonconformists couldn't hold any public office and, significantly for Isaac, they couldn't go to either of the universities (there were only two in the country at the time). So, when Isaac left school and someone offered to arrange for him to study at Oxford or Cambridge, he had to decide what to do. Since going would have meant having to conform, Watts declined.

Instead of going to university, Isaac went to the non-conformist equivalent. These were called 'dissenting academies' (nonconformists were also called dissenters, because they dissented from the established church). Watts went to one in Stoke Newington, which is now in north London but back then was a village just outside London. Watts studied there for four years under the main tutor, Thomas Rowe. If you think this might have been the soft option compared to university, think again! Isaac writes in his notebook:

> 1690. Left the grammar-school, and came to London to Mr Rowe's, to study philosophy, etc.

Those last two words cover more than you might think. The academy studied philosophy and a lot more. The curriculum included Latin, Greek, Hebrew, maths, history, geography, natural science, logic, rhetoric, ethics, metaphysics, anatomy, law and theology. Watts applied himself to his studies with vigour and was clearly an able student. However, he probably worked too hard, usually late into the night. This may have caused some permanent health problems, as he later said:

> Midnight studies are prejudicial to nature, and painful experience calls me to repent of the faults of my younger years.[5]

Watts had a couple of study techniques which he later recommended in his works on education. They show us how serious he was about really understanding the topic he was studying. When reading a book, he wrote his own summary of its contents. This, he said, took time, but meant that you remembered what you had read and made further reading on the same topic much easier. Secondly, he interleaved books with blank sheets of paper so that he could write notes, make additional comments and cross-reference other works. One of these interleaved books is still in existence, and its contents show how much attention he paid to what he was reading.[6]

There was something of a revolution going on in education at the end of the seventeenth century, and Watts was on the cutting edge of it. In previous years, education had had a very traditional basis. There were accepted maxims and truths, and education then worked out from these, trying to apply them logically to different

---

5   Ibid., p. 29.
6   This is now in the Dr Williams' Library in London.

areas. But the Enlightenment had brought a new approach: rather than working from accepted principles, there was new investigation which assumed nothing. Watts later wrote a poem that captured these different approaches and shows us how he felt about them. The poem is called 'Free Philosophy', which was the name given to the new approach because it emphasized a sense of freedom from tradition. The poem begins by criticizing the traditional forms of education:

> Custom, that tyranness of fools,
> That leads the learned round the schools,
> In magic chains of forms and rules!

It later praises Watts' tutor Thomas Rowe:

> I love thy gentle influence, *Rowe*,
> Thy gentle influence like the sun,
> Only dissolves the frozen snow,
> Then bids our thoughts like rivers flow,
> And choose the channels where they run.[7]

Here is the freedom to think new thoughts. Rowe was well known for allowing and encouraging this new investigation. However, this raised a tension: what happens if this new freedom means you start thinking that tradition is wrong in matters of faith?

Watts wrote a letter while at the academy that gives us an example of exactly this problem. He says that we should be subject only to what God says in the Scriptures, as his father taught him, and comments on the part our reason should play:

> In matters of the Christian faith, I would make the Scripture my guide ... My reason should be used as a necessary instrument to compare the several parts of revelation together, to discover their mutual explication, as well as to judge whether they run counter to any dictates of natural light.

---

7   Watts, *Works*, 'Horae Lyricae', Volume 4, p. 393.

So, reason is a helpful instrument in understanding Scripture. But then Watts comments on what happens if reason is let loose in free thinking:

> But if an inquisitive mind overleaps the bounds of faith, and give the reins to all our reasonings upon divine themes in so wide and open a field as that of all possibles and probables, it is no easy matter to guess where they will stop their career.

So, if you let your reason run where it likes, it could take you anywhere! He then gives an example on the topic of Jesus' divinity:

> I have made experiment of this in my own meditations; when I have given my thoughts a loose, and let them rove without confinement, sometimes I seem to have carried reason with me even to the camp of Socinius; but then St. John gives my soul a twitch, and St. Paul bears me back again (if I mistake not his meaning) almost to the tents of John Calvin.[8]

When Watts refers to the 'camp of Socinius', he means the heresy started by a theologian of that name (usually called Socinianism). Among other things, Socinius denied that Jesus was truly God. Watts is, therefore, saying that his free thinking could carry him to deny Jesus' divinity, but then the Bible (in the form of John and Paul) pulls him back to the straight and narrow (as represented by John Calvin, the sixteenth-century reformer). This shows that Watts knew the dangers of free thinking: he gives the 'experiment' above as an example of what might happen when people 'overleap the bounds of faith'.

This tension between the use of reason and submission to Scripture was a crucial topic in Watts' day. The eighteenth century saw many Christians slide away from the gospel, saying that Jesus wasn't truly God precisely because of this issue. Many ended up as Unitarians who denied the doctrine of the Trinity. In a later chapter we'll

---

8   Ibid., 'Reliquiae Juveniles', Volume 4, p. 532.

examine more of what Watts says about this and how he tried to resolve the issue himself.

After his time at the academy, Watts returned home for a while. His notebook simply says: 'Dwelt at my father's house 2 years & ¼. 1694.' We do not know exactly what he spent his time doing. An early biographer refers to a period of meditation and prayer, but at some point writing hymns came into play. At the time, people mainly sang metrical psalms. These were hymns based on the psalms in the Old Testament, and the idea was to keep as close to the original psalm as possible. The poetry involved was pretty hard going, with stilted lyrics and difficult syntax.

The story of Watts' beginnings as a hymn writer is as follows: on return from church one Sunday, Isaac complained to his father about the terrible hymns they had to sing. His dad wisely responded, 'If you don't like them that much, why don't you write something better yourself?' So, he did! It seems that they sang a new hymn that evening that had just been composed by the younger Watts. It was based on Revelation 5:9, which describes singing a new song to Jesus, the Lamb who was slain. The first verse ran like this:

> Behold the glories of the Lamb
> Amidst His Father's throne.
> Prepare new honours for His Name,
> And songs before unknown.[9]

Notice this is not just a new hymn. It's a new hymn about singing new songs to Jesus! It seems that after this Watts spent significant time writing more and more of these new hymns. We'll look at why and how he wrote his hymns in a later chapter.

Becoming a teacher

After this period of time at home, Watts began a new job as a private tutor in a well-to-do family. The family was that of Sir John Hartopp and his wife Elizabeth. Sir John

---

9   Watts' hymns are available in his collected works (vol. 4) but also in a variety of other books and online.

Hartopp was a Member of Parliament for Leicestershire. He and Elizabeth had six children, and Watts was responsible for their education. The Hartopps lived in Stoke Newington, and so Watts returned to where he had studied. While he was with the Hartopp family, he attended the church they belonged to: a Congregationalist church meeting in Mark Lane, in what is now the financial heart of London. Back then it was a street of large houses, the homes of rich city merchants. On his twenty-fourth birthday, 17 July 1698, Watts preached his first sermon. He began to preach occasionally on trips home to Southampton as well. The Hartopps also had an estate near Melton Mowbray in Leicestershire, and Watts would sometimes travel there with them and then conduct services in the meeting house in the village of Freeby. Watts was later pictured in a stained-glass window in that building along with Mary Hartopp, one of the children he taught.

This was a time when Watts not only taught but also continued to study and started to write. He wrote a number of educational works to help him in his tutoring. The reason was simple: he couldn't find books that covered the material he thought was important, and so he wrote them himself. These 'study manuals' for his students were later lengthened and published. Some, like a book on astronomy, simply covered the topic in a helpful and straightforward way. Others, like a book on logic, were so good that they became textbooks at the universities at Oxford, Cambridge, and Yale, as well as at the dissenting academies across the country.

By the time his role as tutor ended, Watts was still twenty-four. He was a convinced nonconformist who had known suffering for his family's convictions. He was bright and well educated, and had started to navigate the troubled waters of how revealed religion should relate to the new Enlightenment view of reason. He was a gifted poet who had started to write hymns to change the praise of his church. He was an educator able to write simply and well. He was also a preacher; and it is on this last role that his life was now to focus.

2
WATTS THE PASTOR

Starting in ministry

As we saw in the last chapter, by his mid-twenties Watts was working as tutor to the Hartopp family and he was attending the same church as them – a congregation meeting in Mark Lane in the centre of London. But Watts' notebook of significant events in his life suddenly says:

> Feb 1699   Preached as Dr Chauncy's Assistant in the Church at Mark Lane, & a little after that my fever and weakness began.

Watts had ceased being a tutor and become a pastor.

The congregation at Mark Lane included some well-off and well-known families – it comprised the aristocratic end of nonconformity. The Hartopps were a good example of this. Sir John Hartopp was a Member of Parliament but a convinced dissenter. In fact, during the reign of James II, he was fined over £7,000 for his nonconformity. He used to take notes on sermons preached in the morning at Mark Lane and then read them to his household in the evening.

As the note above says, the pastor of the Mark Lane church was Dr Chauncy, and Watts joined him as an assistant and began preaching regularly. Dr Chauncy was a learned and able pastor, but he was not popular, and the church was not doing well under his leadership. The source of the trouble is variously traced to his stubbornness in controversy, his learned but tedious preaching on theological controversy or his focus on rigid church discipline. It may, of course, have been a combination of these factors. Whatever the cause, the relationship between the congregation and Dr Chauncy was going downhill and, two years after Watts had become assistant pastor, Chauncy resigned and became a tutor in a dissenting academy.

Following his resignation, the congregation first began to look for a replacement, with Watts staying as assistant pastor. As the search for a new pastor went on, though, the suggestion was made that Watts himself take over. However, as the notebook entry above indicates, Watts was not well. His notebook entry for June 1701, just after Chauncy had stepped down, reads: 'Went to Bath by the advice of Physicians'. This was the common tactic of the day to escape the city and benefit from the clean air of the country and the waters at Bath.

Hence, while the church was considering calling Watts as their pastor, they had to note in the minutes of a church meeting that Watts was 'under continued indispositions of body and weakness in the country' and that he had 'given us but little encouragement to expect his return among us'.[1] This was the start of a pattern of illness that would continue throughout Watts' life.

The church responded by holding a day of prayer and fasting specifically for the 'restoration of Mr Watts' health and for the provision of a pastor for this Church.' These two requests were obviously connected! Watts did recover and returned to London, having been away for five months. The church now called Watts to be the new pastor. He hesitated, citing his weakness which meant he was unable to preach twice each Sunday. The congregation persisted, though, and eventually Watts accepted the position. He wrote to the church again, pointing out his weakness once again, but saying:

---

1   These notes and others following are from a church register. Details are given in Arthur Paul Davis, *Isaac Watts: His Life and Works* (London: Independent Press, 1948), p. 247.

But your perseverance in your choice and love, your constant profession of edification by my ministry, the great probability you show of building up this famous and decayed church of Christ, if I accept the call, and your prevailing fears of its dissolution if I refuse, have given me ground to believe that the voice of this church is the voice of Christ by you ...

I accept your call, promising in the presence of God and his saints, my utmost diligence in all the duties of a pastor, so far as God shall enlighten and strengthen me; and I leave this promise in the hands of Christ our Mediator, to see it performed by me unto you through the assistance of his grace and Spirit.[2]

He was ordained as pastor on 18 March 1702. The ordination sermon was preached by Thomas Rowe, Watts' tutor from the dissenting academy. He preached on Jeremiah 3:15, 'And I will give you pastors according to mine (my) heart, which shall feed you with knowledge and understanding' (KJV).

Life as pastor and writer

In the process of being appointed as pastor, Watts wrote to the congregation at Mark Lane to explain his views on a number of topics. One example is that of church discipline, which we should remember seems to have been a significant point of friction with the former pastor, Dr Chauncy. On this topic, Watts wisely said that he had found the works of John Owen of considerable help, but also the works of Dr Chauncy himself. In other words, he wasn't about to operate in a different way from his predecessor.

Within this letter Watts speaks about his view of the role of pastor in a local church:

The duties of a pastor are chiefly such as these: preaching and labouring in the word and doctrine; praying earnestly for his flock in public and private; administering the seals of the covenant of grace, baptism, and the Lord's supper; being ready in season and out of season, teaching and

---

2   Gibbons, *Memoirs*, p. 99.

exhorting, comforting and rebuking with all long-suffering and doctrine; contending for and preserving the truth; approving himself an example to the flock; visiting the sick and the poor; praying with them and taking care of them; making inquiries into the state of his flock, especially as to spiritual affairs; endeavouring to stir up and promote religion in their households and families; and labouring, by all means and methods of Christ's appointment, to further their faith and holiness, their comfort and increase.[3]

This reflects some of the focus on a 'one-man ministry' which was typical of the day; however, it is still a wonderful picture of pastoral ministry.

We don't know a great deal about Watts' early years as pastor. We do know that at this time he moved from the Hartopps' house in Stoke Newington into the city itself. Presumably, this was a better location from which to function as pastor. He lived in the house of Thomas Hollis, another wealthy nonconformist, from 1702 to 1710.

We also know that Watts' poor health continued after his appointment. His notebook says that he was 'seized with violent jaundice and cholic' and 'had a very slow recovery – eight or nine weeks' illness'. This resulted in the church calling an assistant pastor to help in the ministry and to take over when Watts was unable to function. Samuel Price was appointed in this role in 1703. Later that year, Watts also started to employ someone to read and write for him, acting as a personal assistant in his studies. The reason was because of 'my great indispositions of body and weakness of head'. However, Watts then enjoyed a sustained period of reasonably good health over much of the next decade and was able to minister without significant interruptions.

The result was significant growth in the church. In 1704, two years after he took over, the congregation relocated their Sunday meetings to Pinner's Hall. This seems to have been required because the building in Mark Lane was rather dilapidated. However, Pinner's Hall was certainly

---

3   Thomas Milner, *The Life, Times and Correspondence of the Rev. Isaac Watts, D.D.* (London: Simpkin and Marshall, 1834), p. 181.

larger, and so the move may also have been made in order to accommodate increased attendance. Four years later, the church moved again to a newly built meeting-house in Bury Street. This new building could seat 428 people. That's a significant number, given that there were roughly sixty members when Watts took over.

Watts was also starting to be known as an author – both in poetry and prose. In 1705, his poems were published. Then, in 1707, an essay entitled *Against Uncharitableness* was printed and, later that year, his famous book of *Hymns and Spiritual Songs*.

It is significant that Watts' first prose work was on 'uncharitableness'. This tells us something about his personality. He hated to see division in the church and he wrote this work to encourage people not to separate unnecessarily on disputed matters of doctrine. He said that charity is the greatest of virtues among men, the one in which we are most like God, and that uncharitableness is the worst of vices, in which we are like the devil.

This desire for unity among Christians continued throughout Watts' life. It seems to have come from a personality that shrank from controversy and desired concord, but also from the conviction that Christians can and should agree over the fundamentals of the faith, and need not fall out over minor doctrines. This desire for unity was shown in Watts' friendships: while disagreeing with Anglicans over various points, Watts was friendly with many prominent Anglican leaders, including the Bishop of London.

Watts was becoming a recognized leader in dissent. This is shown by his being invited to give a public sermon in 1707 to the 'Societies for Reformation of Manners'. These were societies that campaigned for reformation in the morality of the country, such as laws against drunkenness. As was common in his day, while Watts did not think the state should enforce religion on people, he did think there should be enforcement of morality.

Watts' publications resulted in what seems to have been his only attempt at romance. A lady called Elizabeth

Singer had read Watts' poetry and loved it, so much so that she wanted to meet the author. However, Watts was not an attractive man: he was short, sallow-faced, hook-nosed and pale. Miss Singer, by contrast, was beautiful. They did meet, and it seems that Watts was smitten and eventually proposed to her. Her reply has to go down as one of the best rejections in history: 'Mr Watts, I only wish I could say that I admire the casket as much as I admire the jewel.'[4] In other words – you're great, but too ugly! Miss Singer married someone else but continued as a friend of Watts, and he later edited and published her poetry. Watts would stay single for the rest of his life.

Lethargy and heresy

It is worth pausing to know something of the times in which Watts was ministering. We need to be careful of generalizations, but the bottom line is that the church in the early eighteenth century was in a terrible state. In the Anglican Church, there had been a reaction against the Puritan theology of the seventeenth century which had emphasized sin, the need for new spiritual life, and God's sovereign grace. Now, sermons were lectures on morality and philosophy. It is often said that the preachers were more familiar with Greek philosophers than with the Bible. The result was dry and sleepy religion.

William Hogarth, one of the satirical artists of the day, represented this in an engraving called 'The Sleeping Congregation'. Hogarth depicts a minister preaching, but he has his head buried in his book rather than looking at the congregation. He has clearly been speaking for a long time, because the hourglass next to him has run through. Most of the congregation are fast asleep, even with mouths open to indicate they are snoring. The main exception is a clerk who is taking the opportunity to admire the ample bosom of a sleeping young lady. The text the minister is preaching on is 'Come to me all you who are weary and I will give

---

4   Fountain, *Watts*, p. 45. There are other reports that she had in fact accepted
     someone else's proposal the day before.

you rest'. Here is the uninterested and ungodly church of the day. It is a caricature but, like all good caricatures, it captures something of reality.

In their doctrine, the Anglican ministers were moving away from the commonly held Puritan positions of the previous generation. The most common first move was to 'Arminianism', which has a greater focus on the role of people rather than God in salvation and godly living. However, this was often a stepping stone to 'Pelagianism', which holds that people can improve by themselves and denies the need for rebirth and renewal by the Holy Spirit. Christianity was becoming a moral self-improvement programme! Along with this were doubts over Jesus' divinity and the doctrine of the Trinity. At worst, Jesus became simply a good example to follow, rather than the Son of God who died for our salvation.

Watts was well aware of these issues, and both preached and wrote about them. We'll look at some of his arguments in later chapters. For now, here is part of a letter to a friend and fellow minister whom Watts was concerned about; he thought he was being taken in by the argument that Christianity was primarily about being moral. Watts says:

> Let me inquire of you, whether you imagine the great and glorious doctrines of the gospel were all contrived, and the affairs themselves transacted, merely to serve a little morality? Whether our great Lord Jesus was incarnate and died, rose and lives, and gave such a gospel, chiefly that we might be just and kind to our neighbours? Or rather, whether the honour of the wisdom, grace and justice of God, the glory of his Son Jesus Christ and the eternal enjoyment of his own love, which his chosen ones obtain thereby, be not far the greater ends of God's contriving the gospel and sending it out among men? And consequently whether these ought not to be insisted on in our preaching at least as much as morality?

> You know me and my way, therefore I talk to you with freedom, and would have the very sense of your soul on

this subject. I could quote St Paul largely for this purpose, but you know his spirit: morality was not the chief ornament of it.[5]

Put simply, did God plan the gospel and the work of Jesus to teach us to be good, or to show us His grace and bring us to enjoy His love, i.e. to save us? The answer is obvious to Watts. Fortunately, the later correspondence shows that the person he is writing to agrees.

Controversy and cul-de-sacs
Things were better in the nonconformist churches, but not by much. The nonconformist churches could be divided into three groups: Presbyterians, Congregationalists and Baptists. The Presbyterians leant towards the same problems as the Anglicans, although not so badly. They tended to focus on morality above God's grace, and some had doubts over Jesus' divinity.

The Congregationalists tended to stick to the gospel more closely, but some were in danger of too great a focus on God's sovereignty and of downplaying people's response to the gospel. This resulted in a controversy over the place of good works in the Christian life. While the Presbyterians tended to emphasize the need for moral change, some Congregationalists went the other way and said it didn't matter how Christians lived, because their sins were forgiven and they had a righteousness given by Jesus.

Watts had already interacted with these issues. In the dissenting academy, he wrote an essay entitled, 'Whether the doctrine of justification by faith alone tends to licentiousness?' In other words, if I'm righteous in Jesus, can I then live disobeying God? His answer was, 'No, of course not!' This was also a feature of his ongoing pastoral ministry. He taught justification by faith alone, which should lead to a godly life.

The Baptists also followed these trends. Some drifted towards morality and making Jesus an example to follow rather than the One who died to make atonement. Others

---

5   Milner, *Watts*, pp. 228-29.

focused on God's sovereignty in similar fashion to the Congregationalists mentioned above. This meant that they lost any evangelistic edge, because they didn't think they should call on people to respond to the gospel. Some said to do so would rob God of His glory in bringing people to faith! But they also had some of their own peculiar theological cul-de-sacs. In particular, there was controversy over Jesus' humanity and divinity. The result was they tended to be inward-looking and to argue among themselves.

Wild imaginings

A very different part of the religious scene was what was called 'enthusiasm'. Enthusiasm was the word used to describe an overly excited or highly emotional religion. This was usually linked to claims of God speaking to people directly and to ecstatic experiences of God. It was similar to some hyper-charismatic claims or experiences we might hear about today.

An example was a group called the 'French Prophets'. As the name suggests, they were a group in France well known for making prophetic claims, and also for mystical experiences. They were persecuted in France, and a group came to London in 1706. They claimed that God was setting up a new age in which He spoke by prophecy; this new dispensation would start in London and spread across the world within three years.

Watts' notebook has this telling entry:

> This year the French Prophets made a great noise in our nation, and drew in Mr Lacy, Sir R Bulkeley, etc. 200 or more had the agitations, 40 had the inspiration. Proved a delusion of Satan at Birmingham. Feb 3 or 4, 1707.

Sir Richard Bulkeley, mentioned here, was a scientist and author. He had a significant curvature of his spine and suffered from ongoing medical problems. He claimed that the French Prophets had cured some of his ailments and wrote a treatise to defend them. The other person, Mr Lacy, left his wife and family to live with one of the women among the prophets, which he justified as what

God wanted by a tortuous use of the Bible. Unfortunately, such ungodly actions, along with their justifications, are not uncommon among this sort of group.

Mr Lacy later predicted that a member of the group, Mr Emms, who was dying, would then be raised from the dead. This led them to delay Mr Emms' funeral until his corpse had begun to rot! Finally, they had to stop waiting for the predicted resurrection and bury him. However, the following year, another member of the group predicted that this same man, Mr Emms, would be raised from his grave (the first predicted resurrection was true, but the expected timing had been wrong!). Mr Lacy spread news of this prophecy in a leaflet, *The Mighty Miracle*, which predicted the date and time of Mr Emms' resurrection.

This caused such a stir that guards were placed around the cemetery where Mr Emms was buried so as to keep public order. The predicted date and time came and went, however, and Mr Emms remained in his grave. Watts wrote in his notebook:

> May 25, 1708. The Prophets disappointed by Mr Emms not rising from the dead.

While these events were extraordinary, they show the other side of the religion of the day: excessive imagination and wild behaviour.

In his preaching, Watts warned people against such 'enthusiasm'. He argued that the Christian life, although supernatural, was not unreasonable or mystical. He accepted that some Christians did have extraordinary experiences and said that these should not be despised. But, he went on, we must not make these typical or expected, and we certainly should never make an experience or an impression a reason to go against God's Word. We'll see more of Watts' arguments about experience in the Christian life later on.

Persecution continues

Nonconformists were now tolerated but not equal members of society. As we've seen, they could not attend university, and public office was closed to them. Some got around this restriction by the practice of 'occasional conformity'. This meant that they would occasionally attend an Anglican church and take the Lord's Supper. In doing so, they had 'conformed' and so could be a Member of Parliament or mayor. However, for the rest of the year they would attend a nonconformist church, which was where their convictions truly lay.

This practice incensed many Tories, one of the two main political parties, which was primarily made up of Anglicans. As a result, the Occasional Conformity Act was passed in 1711. This Act ensured that the practice of occasional conformity no longer provided a loophole by which nonconformists could hold public office. An example was Sir Thomas Abney, who was an 'alderman' of London, with whose family Watts later lived. The Occasional Conformity Act meant Sir Thomas could not attend his nonconformist church and continue as an alderman; but neither was he prepared to conform. He was in the fortunate position of being able to organize private services in his own home, at which Watts would sometimes preach. Watts dedicated two sermons to him, commenting that Abney was at that time 'restrained by the laws of men from public worship in that way you have chosen'.

There were also moments of more significant persecution. One Anglican clergyman who was dead set against nonconformists was Dr Henry Sacheverell. He preached a sermon attacking nonconformists in which he drew comparisons with the execution of King Charles in the previous century and so painted the dissenters as 'fanatic enemies of our Church and Government'. The sermon was so incendiary that Sacheverell was put on trial and subsequently suspended. But his sermon had hit a sore spot and stirred up public outrage against nonconformists. The result was that rioters attacked dissenting meeting-houses. Watts mentions this in his notebook:

> March 1, 1710. The mob rose and pulled down the pews and galleries 6 meeting houses, viz. Mr Burgess, Mr Bradbury, Mr Earle, Mr Wright, Mr Hamilton, and Mr

Ch. Taylor, but were dispersed by the guards under Capt. Horsey at 1 or 2 in the morning.

The pews and pulpits from these meeting-houses were used in bonfires that lit up London at night, and at least a couple of the ministers mentioned by Watts were threatened themselves. All of this reminded the dissenters that theirs was a fragile existence.

That fragility was revealed again with attempts by the high churchmen of Anglicanism to close down the training academies for dissenters such as the one at which Watts had studied. This would mean no higher education for dissenters, with disastrous long-term implications. This was known as the Schism Bill (1714). However, on the very day it was to come into force, Queen Anne died. With her gone, the main proponents of the bill were overthrown and the dissenters breathed a great sigh of relief. They also gave great thanks to God, seeing this as His hand of protection at work.

'Tiresome Sickness'

In 1710, Watts moved house and lived with Mr Bowes, also in the heart of the city. Two years later, however, Watts' health took a significant downturn and he was forced to effectively leave pastoral ministry for the next four years (1712-16). It is never made clear exactly what illness Watts was suffering from. One writer speaks of a 'violent fever which introduced a state of nervous agitation of the most painful and distressing kind.'[6] It seems that at times he had hallucinations and did not recognize family and friends.

Later, Watts wrote a poem about his illness, selected lines from which give us a feel for some of what he went through.

> If I but close my eyes, strange images
> In thousand forms and thousand colours rise.
> Stars, rainbows, moons, green dragons, bears, and ghosts;

---

6   Ibid., p. 299.

An endless medley rush upon the stage,
And dance and riot wild in Reason's court,
Above control. I'm a raging storm,
Where seas and skies are blended; while my soul,
Like some light worthless chip of floating cork,
Is tossed from wave to wave: now high-mounted on the ridge
With breaking floods, I drown, and seem to lose,
All being.

This period of illness is noted in the epitaph on Watts' gravestone, which he had composed himself. It refers to 'fifty years of feeble labours in the Gospel, interrupted by four years of tiresome sickness...'

With Watts out of action, his assistant Samuel Price was appointed as a full co-pastor in 1713. This was very much with Watts' approval. The two men seemed to get on well. In his will, Watts would later refer to him as a faithful friend and companion in the labours of ministry. In Watts' letters to the church while he was ill, he often commended Price to them as one whose ministry 'shall ever endear him both to you and to me'.

This sickness resulted in Watts moving house again, in what was to be a significant move. He was invited by Sir Thomas Abney to his home in Hertfordshire, again on the premise that the quiet of the country would help Watts' recovery. Sir Thomas was a successful businessman – he was one of the first directors of the Bank of England – and, as we mentioned above, an alderman. He was also a generous benefactor and zealous Christian.

Watts was, in fact, to spend the rest of his life in the various homes of the Abneys. Later in life, when Lady Huntingdon visited Watts, he told her that she was arriving on a remarkable day. When asked what that was, Watts replied, 'This very day thirty years ago I came hither, to the house of my good friend Sir Thomas Abney, intending to spend but a single week under this friendly roof; and I have extended my visit to the length of exactly thirty years.' His presence was clearly welcomed, though, because Lady Abney responded, 'Sir, what you term a long thirty year visit, I consider as the shortest visit my family ever received.'

While in the Abney house, Watts took up the role of tutor to the various children. He would act as 'chaplain' within the house, conducting occasional Sunday evening services and preaching. By 1716, Watts was able to return to his role as pastor, but his health was never to be the same again. We'll reflect in a later chapter on how he responded to his illnesses and what lessons he learned. As Watts returned to ministry, though, some of the heresies of the day were making greater inroads and were about to cause public division.

3
REASONABLE FAITH

The first half of the eighteenth century is often called 'The Age of Reason'. That's too simplistic as an overall description, but it does capture the fact that reason was lifted up to new heights. The 'Enlightenment' was changing the culture of the day so that rather than relying on tradition, religion or superstition, people looked to reason as a source of truth and guidance in how to live.

This newfound confidence in reason was bolstered by great advances in science. This was the age of Isaac Newton and his revolutionary discoveries of the movement of the planets. The Royal Society had been started in the previous century and regularly produced explanations of things that people had previously not understood. These sorts of scientific advances made people feel that reason, properly applied, could explain everything.

But how should reason be used? The philosopher John Locke was hugely influential in this discussion through his book called *An Essay Concerning Human Understanding*. This work presented a system in which one only believed what was 'reasonable' i.e. what made sense in one's head. He gave rules as to how to think and hence what could be known. His system gave a rational approach to thinking and learning. It is difficult for us to appreciate this today, but the result was the dawning of a new age and a confidence in reason that had never been seen before.

This had a huge effect on religion. Previous authorities in religion had been *tradition*, believing what people had always believed, or *church authorities* (such as the Pope), whose word was thought to be binding. There had also been those who followed *personal experience* or the *inner light* of the Spirit. This had resulted in breakaway groups such as the Quakers. But now, instead of all of these, the authority of reason was lifted high.

As a result of this shift, people were keen to present themselves and their beliefs as 'reasonable'. This wasn't necessarily taken to be a threat to the faith, for ministers believed the gospel was perfectly reasonable and was itself supported by reason. In fact, many ministers welcomed the new thinking and thought it would be easier to now prove the truth of Christianity.

Not only was there a pull towards being 'reasonable'; there was also a reaction against what was seen as the 'unreasonable enthusiasm' of the previous century. The Puritan era in the seventeenth century had resulted in both a revolution and the execution of a king. That was taken as proof positive that England needed a calmer, more tolerant, and reasonable religion.

At first, this was not considered a problem – in fact, everyone thought it was good and reasonable! Among orthodox ministers, Scripture was still seen as the ultimate authority. However, it was now Scripture as understood by reason. A significant move had taken place: reason had been given the upper hand; it was the ultimate guide. This was eventually to have devastating results.

Watts and John Locke

We mentioned John Locke above – he embodied the new rationality and his *An Essay Concerning Human Understanding* became the rationalists' 'bible' of his day. He wrote another significant book called *The Reasonableness of Christianity*. As the title suggests, this argued that the Christian faith is entirely reasonable, but it also watered down the content of the faith.

Watts interacted with Locke many times in his works, producing some of the most significant engagements with his thought in the early eighteenth century. In these writings, we see Watts as a philosopher/theologian arguing about the right role of reason in the Christian faith. Watts had a very high view of Locke. With regard to Locke's most significant work, Watts says:

> His essay on the human understanding has diffused fairer light through the world in numerous areas of science and of human life. There are many admirable chapters in that book, and many truths in them, which are worthy of letters of gold.[1]

In agreeing with Locke, Watts takes on board much of the new logic of the Enlightenment. He wasn't a man to give a knee-jerk reaction of rejection. Remember the training in the academy about 'freedom of thought'? That meant that he willingly interacted with new ideas. However, he didn't buy the new thinking hook, line and sinker; he also had his criticisms. In this chapter, we'll look at Watts' view of the role of reason and how he defended the faith as 'reasonable'.

Watts and reason

Watts wrote a number of works about the use of reason. The most general was a book simply called *Logic*. We previously mentioned this was used as a textbook in dissenting academies and at Oxford, Cambridge and Yale. We get a feel for what it covers in the long subtitle:

> The right use of reason in the inquiry after truth, with a variety of rules to guard against error in the affairs of religion and human life, as well as in the sciences.

In his *Logic*, Watts happily spoke about the advances made in science and reason, and embraced them. He said that for us to only ever believe what people before us have believed is to enslave ourselves in tradition. Thus, he speaks positively about the advances made by philosophers and scientists such as Bacon, Descartes, Copernicus, Newton, Locke and Boyle, saying:

---

1   Watts, *Works*, 'Philosophical Essays', Volume 5, p. 503.

> We must all act according to the best of our own light, and the judgement of our own consciences, using the best advantages which providence has given us, with an honest and impartial diligence to enquire and search out the truth. For every one of us must give an account of himself to God.[2]

Notice that Watts is positive about the use of reason and about impartial enquiry into truth. Also notice that he thinks that the advances in science and logic in his day are because of God's providence. And, lastly, notice that he thinks that we will one day give an account to God of what we have believed and done. So, he is positive about the Enlightenment, but wants to bring its advances under the rule of God.

As was standard in his age, Watts thought God had given us two 'springs of light', that is, 'reason and revelation'. As God has given them both to us, they cannot contradict themselves or each another. Watts says: 'There is not any one part of divine revelation which is really inconsistent with reason or with any other parts of revelation itself.'[3] Watts also said that we have to use our reason to understand revelation in the first place.

Virtually everyone would agree with this. The real questions emerge when you ask what this looks like in practice. What do you do when something the Bible teaches appears to be 'unreasonable'? What do you do when you think one part of the Bible contradicts another? What do you say to someone who thinks they can know all they need to from reason by itself? We'll return to these questions.

Reason the governor gone wrong

Watts believed God has made us as thinking, feeling and acting people, but it is our reason that should direct and control us. Our reason allows us to both understand and evaluate, and should act like the steering wheel on life, directing where we go and what we do. Watts says:

---

2   Ibid., 'Logic', Volume 5, p. 111.
3   Ibid., 'Ruin and Recovery', Volume 6, p. 179.

The understanding, which perceives the fitness or unfitness, good or evil of things, should be a director or guide to the other power which is active, i.e. the will, that it may regulate and determine its actions wisely, and choose and refuse objects proposed to it according to the fitness or unfitness, good or evil which is discovered by the understanding.[4]

So, Watts believed that Adam and Eve's reason would have been perfect and would have led them to live rightly before God. However, reason has gone wrong and the blame is laid at the door of our sinful desires. Watts believes that we *could* reason correctly, but as we try to do so, envy, anger, fear, lust and many other desires lead us astray. He says:

The various passions or affections of the mind are numerous and endless springs of prejudice. They disguise every object they converse with, and put their own colours upon it, and thus lead the judgement astray from truth.[5]

The result is that our reason is clouded and we cannot think properly. As Watts puts it:

The eye of the understanding is strangely blinded, and the judgment strangely perverted by the fall of man; we are led into false judgments of things by the corruptions of our minds, by the unhappy influence that present perceived things have over our whole nature, and the empire which appetite and evil passions have gotten over our superior faculties.[6]

Another way of saying this is that, as we think about our careers, pride and ambition distort our thinking; as we think about our possessions, desire for comfort shapes our response; and as we think about relationships, envy and lust override what we should know to be true.

The result for Watts is that there are great limits put on reason. This is where he differs from John Locke. Locke

---

4   Ibid., 'Freedom of Will', Volume 6, p. 385.
5   Ibid., 'Logic', Volume 5, p. 176.
6   Ibid., 'Philosophical Essays', Volume 5, p. 552.

had argued that reason could tell us everything we really needed to know – while he accepted that revelation from God was still of some use. We can see this in a test case: what information is available to someone who never hears the gospel? Locke answered that such a person had the light of reason, and if they used it properly, they could discover the way to God. He assumed that reason would lead us to realize there was a God, and that we were sinners, and that God would forgive us if we asked Him. That might seem odd to us but simply shows the great confidence people had in reason at the time.

But Watts disagreed! Watts wrote a book called *The Strength and Weakness of Human Reason*, which investigated what reason could and could not tell us. Could it lead us to repentance and faith? He said 'No', because sin had fatally wounded our powers of reason. As we saw above, the problem was not so much that reason itself didn't work properly but that sinful desires led it astray. As a result, Watts admitted that there was a hypothetical possibility that reason could lead us to the truth but that in practice it never would. He argues:

> ... though there be a natural sufficiency in human reason to find out such a religion as might save them, yet it is ten thousand to one, if they ever duly and rightly exercise it.[7]

In preaching on this topic, Watts said that our reason could only lead to a 'feeling after God in the dark, than a sight of him in daylight', and uncertainty and many mistakes about God must result. So, despite its potential, the light of reason is so poor that knowing God through it is impossible.

In these arguments, Watts is showing that he is a product of his age. He still has a very high view of reason. He even thinks that reason by itself is relatively unaffected by sin; the problem only comes when sinful desires overwhelm reason. This leads Watts to call on people to be unbiased and impartial in their judgments. He thought if we

---

7   Ibid., 'Strength and Weakness', Volume 2, p. 248.

restrained our sinful desires, we would allow our reason to function properly. However, he also thought that our sinful desires were so strong that we were unable to do that.

In holding this position, Watts hadn't completely captured the Biblical view of how reason itself is affected by the Fall. Although we claim to be wise, we actually become foolish, and sin distorts the way we think (see Rom. 1:21-23). So Watts probably had too high a view of reason – which we will see again later. This was perhaps inevitable, or at least not surprising, given the culture in which he lived. However, he did rightly see that sin meant reason was limited and could not lead us to God – he arrived at the right conclusion even if we might want to change his argument.

The need for revelation

Watts believed that, since reason was blinded by sin, we had a desperate need for God to reveal Himself to us. This He does through the Bible. Hence, in an age which was constantly relying on reason, Watts persistently argued for the importance of revelation. He says:

> ... the revelation of God in an illustrious manner supplies the deficiencies of our reason, and enlightens our natural darkness in the knowledge of divine things ...[8]

This means that we rejoice that God has revealed Himself to us and we hold the authority of the Bible over everything else. Thus, Watts said it is revelation 'to which I entirely submit my faith and practice'.

We see this summarized in some of Watts' hymns. One hymn speaks first of how we can know something of God from creation and our reason:

> Nature with open volume stands,
> To spread her Maker's praise abroad,
> And ev'ry labour of his hands,
> Shows something worthy of a God:

---

8   Ibid., 'Ruin and Recovery', Volume 6, p. 180.

But it continues, saying that we only see God's glory fully in the cross:

> But in the grace that rescued man,
> His brightest form of glory shines;
> Here, on the cross, 'tis fairest drawn
> In precious blood and crimson lines.

The next verse begins, 'Here his whole name appears complete', showing that the revelation of God is only known fully through Jesus Christ.

Watts wrote several poems about John Locke. In one, Watts chides Locke for his confidence in reason. He speaks of how reason can indeed teach some truths but that it is unable to discover core elements of Christian doctrine which God must reveal to us:

> Reason could scarce sustain to see
> The almighty one, the eternal three,
> Or bear the infant deity;
> Scarce could her pride descend to own
> Her Maker stooping from his throne,
> And dressed in glories so unknown.
> A ransomed world, a bleeding God,
> And heaven appeased with flowing blood,
> Were themes too painful to be understood.[9]

Reason and the Spirit

While revelation is desperately needed to bring light in our darkness, it doesn't do away with our reason. Watts uses an analogy to explain this:

> In this matter reason is the eye, true religion is the object: all other helps, divine and human, are as the light, as spectacles, etc. Now it is impossible to see with anything but our own eyes, i.e. our reason. Yet a clear light is also necessary, without which our eye cannot see the object, nor our reason find out the true religion.[10]

---

9 Ibid., 'Horae Lyricae', Volume 4, p. 397.

10 Milner, *Watts*, p. 125.

In other words, we cannot know anything without using our reason, just like we cannot see anything without using our eyes. Yet, we require God's help to see properly – He must shine His light! This means reason still has a great role to play. First of all, reason gives us grounds to believe the gospel and the Bible. Watts says:

> When reason has found out the certain marks or credentials of divine testimony to belong to any proposition, there remains then no further inquiry to be made, but only to find out the true sense and meaning of that which God has revealed, for reason itself demands the belief of it.[11]

In other words, reason helps us to see that the Bible is from God. Once we have seen that, we simply have to discover what it means, and so we use reason to understand what it says. So, we cannot do away with our reason:

> ... the exercise of our reasoning powers is very necessary to assist us, not only in the understanding of the several parts of revelation, but in reconciling them to each other as well as to the dictates of right reason. It is our reason which shows us this blessed harmony.[12]

While insisting on this need to use reason in understanding the Bible properly, Watts also emphasized that we need the work of the Spirit. He believed that the blinding nature of sin was so bad that God's Spirit must open people's eyes for them to see the truth. So he writes to a fellow minister, saying: 'It is God only who can make the consciences of unbelievers hear the voice of reason or revelation.'[13] Similarly:

> We are dark, ignorant and averse to God and all that is holy. We cannot learn divine things, savingly, without the teachings of the Holy Spirit.[14]

---

11 Watts, *Works*, 'Logic', Volume 5, p. 134.
12 Ibid., 'Ruin and Recovery', Volume 6, p. 180.
13 ———, 'Letters,' *Proceedings of the Massachusetts Historical Society* 9 (1894): p. 335.
14 ———, *Works*, 'Caveat against Infidelity', Volume 2, p. 483.

In an age so confident in reason, this was an unwelcome truth. The message of the culture was that if we would only apply ourselves properly to whatever we were studying, then we would understand it fully. Such an approach was brought to the Bible. But Watts insisted that reason alone would never enable us to see the truth of the gospel. Our reason must be used, but God must shine His light. This was most clear in coming to believe the gospel. Watts speaks of the Spirit bringing spiritual sight:

> It is the Spirit who effectively reveals Christ Jesus to the soul as the great reconciler. He discovers who Christ is, and what he has done for us, and sets him before us in all the glories of his mediation. He makes the soul see the all-sufficiency of his sacrifice to atone for sin, the efficacy of his intercession to prevail with God, and his power to save to the uttermost.[15]

This sight of Jesus is not simply *knowing* the truth: the Spirit has to *effectively* reveal Jesus; He has to bring conviction. Watts goes on:

> All the teachings of men, and all the words in the Bible, cannot make a sinful creature see such glory in Christ, such grace, and so desirable salvation, as is done by the enlightening work of the Holy Spirit.[16]

We read an interesting comment on this in a letter from Watts to another minister with whom he studied at the dissenting academy. Watts says that the arguments for the truth of Christianity in his day are utterly convincing: 'never since the apostles' days were equal arguments for Christianity produced.' And yet, he says, 'few are convinced'. His conclusion is:

> I am ready to say that faith, though a rational thing in itself, is yet the gift of God. Not by might of arm, nor by power of argument, but by my Spirit, saith the Lord.[17]

---

15   Ibid., 'Sermons', Volume 1, p. 503.

16   Ibid.

17   ———, 'Letter to Samuel Say, 7 September 1732,' (London: Dr Williams' Library, 1732).

In saying this, Watts was stressing a key Biblical truth at a time when it was in real danger of being rejected.

Reasonable faith

The focus on reason meant there were increasing accusations against the Christian faith. Who could believe in the Trinity, original sin, the incarnation and the atonement? They just weren't reasonable! The result was that many in the church focused on morality rather than on God's acts of salvation. Everyone agreed that morality was reasonable! This move went hand in hand with the changes in doctrine that we saw in the last chapter.

How did Watts respond? He wanted to defend the content of the Christian faith as reasonable – in its original and orthodox forms. First, he defended the principle that believing in revelation doesn't mean being irrational. In a sermon, he says:

> God has given us rational faculties and requires the exercise of them in religious concerns, and he has laid down such grounds for faith in all ages as must approve itself unto reason.[18]

Watts argues that Christians should be familiar with reasons for believing the authority of the Bible, such as prophecies and miracles. He says:

> Endeavour to furnish your minds with such arguments as will justify your own conscience in the belief of the gospel, and will firmly support your profession and practice of it as rational creatures. God requires that a creature of reason should be a reasonable worshipper.[19]

Secondly, Watts defended the central points of Christian doctrine as reasonable. For example, he wrote a book called *Ruin and Recovery*, which explores original sin and atonement through the cross. He picks these two – sin and

---

18   ———, 'Wattiana: Manuscript Remains of the Rev. Isaac Watts, D.D., from the Library of Mr Joseph Parker, his Amanuensis,' (London: British Library), 'Blessedness of Faith without Sight', p. 209.

19   ———, *Works*, 'Caveat against Infidelity', Volume 2, p. 521.

salvation – as cornerstones of the faith. But the subtitle of the book is:

> An Attempt to vindicate the SCRIPTURAL ACCOUNT of these great events upon the plain principles of REASON

This and other of Watts' works try to vindicate what the Bible teaches on the basis of reason. Watts tries to show that the whole narrative of the Bible story makes sense and doesn't involve any contradictions. He does this in a book called *The Harmony of Religion*. He says that this gives:

> ... a compendious arrangement of the discoveries of the grace of God and the duty of man, in such an order as God has prescribed them, and such as may best show their consistency, their reasonableness and equity.[20]

Notice the last phrase – he wants to show the consistency and reasonableness of the Bible.

As such statements show, Watts wants Christians to think of themselves as perfectly reasonable and perfectly justified in believing traditional Christian doctrine. We see this in a sermon on Romans 1:16, where the apostle Paul speaks of not being ashamed of the gospel. Watts says:

> I am not ashamed to believe this gospel as a man. My rational powers give me no secret reproaches. My understanding and judgment do not reprove and check my faith. ... My own reason approves it, and justifies me in the persuasion and belief of a gospel such as this.[21]

Part of Watts' aim here was good and right. It is good to show that the elements of the gospel don't involve believing contradictions or nonsense. It is helpful to show people that they don't have to throw their brains away in order to be a Christian. It reassures people to see that there are good reasons to believe the Bible.

There was, however, a problem lurking in what Watts was doing. In showing that the gospel is reasonable, he

---

20 Ibid., 'Harmony of Religion', Volume 2, p. 542.

21 Ibid., 'Sermons', Volume 1, p. 166.

could stray into making reason the judge of everything. Reason could take the place of ultimate authority and start to stand over revelation. This is what was happening around him, and Watts was skirting close to the edge. We will see some ways in which this led Watts into dangerous waters in the next chapter. However, there were two key factors in his thought that helped him stay clear of those dangers for the most part.

First, while Watts emphasized that the content of the gospel was reasonable, he also said that some areas of Christian doctrine cannot be properly understood by our reason. That's not because they are unreasonable, but because our reason is limited; therefore, we can't understand them properly. Examples of these were the Trinity (how God is three persons and one God) and the incarnation (how Jesus is fully God and fully man). These are mysteries:

> ... which when revealed unto us, we know merely the existence or reality and certainty of them, but cannot comprehend the manner and mode of how they are.[22]

However, while these are above our comprehension, Watts still insists that it is reasonable to believe in such things: 'Reason itself teaches me to believe some things that are above my understanding.'[23] So, Watts said, when we are faced with clear teaching of Scripture which we cannot explain fully, we are still to affirm that truth. Or, when faced with two propositions from Scripture which we struggle to reconcile, we still affirm them both.

We see a summary of this position in one of Watts' letters. Writing to a lady about why we believe, he says:

> Faith itself is a very rational Grace; it knows what and why it believes, though (as I said before) there are two or three mysteries in our religion proposed to our faith which reason can't comprehend nor easily reconcile, yet faith can give a rational account why it believes them.[24]

22 Ibid., 'Sermons', Volume 1, p. 168.

23 ———, 'Wattiana,' – 'A treatise on the dispositions to be cherished and the means to be employed in the search after religious truth', p. 268.

24 ———, 'Letter to a lady about inward impulses,' (London: British Library).

He goes on to say that Christians should never say that they believe simply because they believe: 'God will not suffer the faith of his Children to become a laughing stock of men and sport of the Carnal World.'

We see the limitation of reason expressed in Watts' hymns. A hymn entitled 'Divine glories above our reason' includes the following verse:

Our reason stretches all its wings,
And climbs above the skies;
But still how far beneath thy feet
Our grov'lling reason lies!

Reason can fly high; but it never gets close to God!

Similarly, in a hymn entitled 'Song of praise to the blessed Trinity', the last verse reads:

Almighty God to thee
Be endless honours done,
The undivided Three,
And the mysterious One:
Where reason fails
With all her pow'rs,
Their faith prevails
And love adores.

Where reason fails, faith gains access. More than that, such truths which we cannot understand become reasons for love and adoration.

Reasonable experiences

The second position that kept Watts back from a dangerous dependence on reason was his view of Christian experience. We've noted the background of 'enthusiasm' in the eighteenth century. Enthusiasts claimed God was speaking to them individually, usually also claiming to have ecstatic experiences of God. Enthusiasm was the opposite of being 'reasonable'.

Watts had no desire to defend enthusiasm. In fact, he speaks of it as 'the land of blind enthusiasm, that region of clouds and darkness, that pretends to divine light'.

However, while Watts criticized enthusiasm, he also wanted to promote real, heartfelt Christianity. In his first volume of published sermons, Watts chose to focus on the heartfelt nature of true religion. He says in the preface that he has done this because he believes this is not properly emphasized in his day, and he wants to:

> ...rescue those arguments from the charge of enthusiasm and to put them in such a light as might show their perfect consistence with common sense and reason.[25]

In other words, Watts wants to keep the inward reality of heartfelt faith but also to defend this as reasonable. He is trying to justify a faith which includes our hearts in the face of a culture that is only about using our minds. In doing this, Watts is well aware that he could himself be branded an enthusiast. However, he argues back, saying that there is nothing odd or weird about saying that God's Spirit at work in us would result in our feeling! He says:

> There is nothing in all this account of things but what is perfectly agreeable to the word of God, and to the rational actions of created minds, under the happy influences of the uncreated Spirit.[26]

In other words, the work of the Spirit should result in our feeling guilt over sin or joy over salvation, and that is both true to God's Word and to reason.

Watts defends his position by giving some examples of people who have spoken of their experience of God and argues that they would never be considered enthusiasts themselves. His main example is the earlier Puritan minister John Howe. He says that no one who knew him would accuse him of wild imagination. Rather, he is well known in the following way:

> ... a person whose solid sense, whose deep sagacity, whose sedate judgement, and the superior excellence of his

---

25 ———, *Works*, 'Sermons', Volume 1, p. xxii.
26 Ibid., 'Evangelical Discourses', Volume 2, p. 91.

reasoning powers, leave no room to charge him with vain and delusive raptures of a heated imagination.[27]

So Watts says – just because we have a high view of reason doesn't mean we should have a low view of experience. Just because we believe Christians should think clearly doesn't mean they shouldn't feel deeply. This was a desperately needed note to sound in a cool, rational age.

But Watts would go further. Just as he argued that Christian doctrine can go beyond the comprehension of reason, he said, so Christian experience can go beyond it as well. We can have experiences of God which we cannot properly explain. So, God may give people a 'powerful and pleasant sense' that they are His. They may be 'raised to holy raptures, to heavenly joy and assurance.' Such experiences can be the product of our imagination, and Watts warns people about that. However, he also wants to say that that need not necessarily be the case.

This focus on the experience of the believer is then where Watts directs people for assurance. So, when Watts preaches a sermon on 'The rational defence of the gospel', he concludes by saying that the gospel comes with 'such solid grounds and foundations as justifies its highest promises and proposals to the reason of men.' It is perfectly reasonable. However, he goes on to say that the final assurance for the Christian is experience of God in the transforming power of the gospel:

> Learn hence the true method of obtaining Christian courage … It is by getting it wrought in your hearts and lives by Christian experience, and not by learning a mere form of words in a road of education and catechism. You must feel it as the power of God to your salvation, or you will never suffer much for it.[28]

We see his position in a hymn Watts wrote to accompany this sermon:

---

27   Ibid., 'Evangelical Discourses', Volume 2, p. 97.

28   Ibid., 'Sermons', Volume 1, p. 192.

Jesus thy witness speaks within;
The mercy which thy words reveal,
Refines the heart from sense and sin
And stamps its own celestial seal.

Learning and wit may cease their strife,
When miracles with glory shine;
The voice that calls the dead to life
Must be almighty and divine.

We'll look at Watts' view of heart religion in more detail in a later chapter. For now, I simply want to focus on what Watts is doing in responding to the 'reasonable' voice of the day. He is defending our experience of God. He wants Christians to know the joy of salvation, the assurance of adoption and the knowledge of God's love. He wants believers not to be ashamed of such things in a day when 'reason' is everything. Reasonable Christianity was too often cool and dry Christianity. In response, Watts happily defends the reasonableness of the faith *and* the reasonableness of Christian experience.

Summary

In recent years, Christian leaders such as Timothy Keller and William Lane Craig have encouraged Christians to know why they believe and what they believe. They have spoken of 'the reason for God', or 'reasonable faith'. They have helpfully interacted with criticisms of Christianity and challenged the scepticism of unbelievers. This is what is called 'apologetics'. Not apologizing for the faith, but giving reasons for it, showing why it should be believed.

Watts, then, was an eighteenth-century apologist.

He responded to the thinking of his day not by rejecting it totally, nor by swallowing it unthinkingly. Instead, he tried to take on board what was good and helpful but also to critique what was undesirable. He is a good model for us in this.

He is a good model too in that he enters the battle where it is raging and tries to show people that Christianity is perfectly reasonable. But he doesn't forget to insist on key truths which it would have been easy to forget – such as the need for the work of the Spirit. He also doesn't enter the battle entirely on the opposition's terms. If he had, he would have only spoken of reason. Instead, he also spoke about experience.

Watts did buy into his culture's view of reason too much. That's easy for us to see from where we stand. It is much harder when you're in the middle of the battle. And in the last analysis, he stood against the overdependence on reason of his day. In an essay on the content of the gospel, Watts reflects on the errors that were being multiplied around him because of a high view of reason. He responds:

> Now, perhaps, some may think it the duty and business of the day to temporise, and by preaching the gospel a little more conformably to natural religion, in a mere rational or legal form, to bring it down as near as may be to their scheme, that we may gain them to hear and approve it, or at least, that we may not offend them. But I am rather of the opinion, that we should in such a day stand up for the defence of the gospel in the full glory of its most important doctrines, and in the full freedom of its grace; that we should preach it in its most divine and most evangelical form, that the cross of *Christ*, by the promised power of the Spirit, may vanquish the vain reasoning of men, and that this despised doctrine triumphing in the conversion of souls, may confound the wise and the mighty, and silence the disputers of this world.[29]

---

29   Ibid., 'Orthodoxy and Charity', Volume 3, p. 603.

4
DEFENDING THE FAITH

We've seen that Watts was living and ministering at a time of theological drift. There are heresies and errors throughout church history, so that shouldn't surprise us. What changes is how significant the errors are and how badly the church is infected by them. For Watts, the first half of the eighteenth century saw significant errors badly affecting the church!

Debating the Trinity

We've already considered the great rise in people's confidence in reason. One of the main casualties of this shift was the doctrine of the Trinity. Christians had always said that they believed in one God in three persons. This had been explained in various ways but also had simply been accepted as one of the 'mysteries' of the faith. For many, this became a chink in the armour of 'reasonable Christianity'. It simply didn't make sense and so had to be adapted and changed.

Two theological changes appeared in the late seventeenth century and flowed over into the eighteenth. The first is called 'Arianism', after a false teacher in the early church (Arius). Arianism taught that Jesus was a god but a lesser god than the Father. This allowed people to say that there was really only one person who was properly God, and so the problem of the Trinity was immediately sorted: there was only one true God, the Father. The Holy Spirit simply became God's active power in the world, who wasn't a person in His own right, and Jesus was this lesser being created by the Father. Jehovah's Witnesses today believe something very similar to this.

The second change was called Socinianism. Socinians didn't think Jesus was any kind of god at all. In fact, they didn't think He even existed until His birth. They denied that Jesus' death was to save us and bring forgiveness and instead believed that Jesus lived a good life as an example to us which we should follow. The conclusion was that Christianity was mainly about being good. Of these two, it was Arianism that was obviously closest to the orthodox belief, and it started to make inroads into the church. Various figures within Anglicanism argued for Arianism, or something similar. However, before long this view began to appear in the nonconformist church as well.

The issue came to a head in nonconformity with what was called 'The Salters' Hall Controversy' in 1719. The controversy began in Exeter. A particular minister, with others, was accused of Arian convictions. There was a mixture of both opposition and support for these men in the Exeter region. The church officials weren't sure what to do and so they asked for advice from ministers in London. This resulted in a gathering of Presbyterian, Congregationalist and Baptist ministers at Salters' Hall to debate the issue. Arianism had been known of for years, but now a group of ministers had to decide what to do when it was found within their own ranks.

The issue may seem simple to us, and in many ways it was to them too. The ministers who gathered believed in the traditional Trinity and they rejected Arianism (although a few may have had some sympathy with it). They also had no desire to allow error to flourish. Why, then, was there a controversy? The issue was over whether people should be *made* to subscribe to a creed or a particular doctrinal position.

There is some important background to remember here – and this illustrates how significant our background and context are for the decisions we make. This group knew of the earlier persecution of dissenters for their unwillingness to conform to the Anglican Church. Watts would have remembered his father being in prison and having to leave home. They still knew personally the experience of discrimination for their nonconformity in not being able to hold public office.

As a result, this group had often argued that Christians should be allowed to decide what to believe for themselves – they had held to 'freedom of conscience' in matters of the faith. They had resisted the imposition of the Anglican creeds as a test because they couldn't sign up to it in every area themselves. So, would they now impose a creed or doctrinal statement on their own ministers? Or would they allow freedom of conscience?

This resulted in a position known as 'no creed but the Bible'. It simply says: I believe the Bible rather than human creeds and theological statements. In one sense, that's obvious, because the Bible is inspired whereas doctrinal statements are not. But the problem is that the Bible is interpreted in different ways by different people. So, what do you do with someone who says they believe the Bible but disagrees that it teaches that Jesus is divine? What if they say they believe the Bible but they also believe that Jesus didn't die to save us from God's punishment? Should we impose creeds to weed out false teachers in the church?

The ministers at Salters' Hall were divided on the issue. Some wanted to impose a statement about the Trinity which all ministers had to agree to as a test of their orthodoxy; others wanted to say that Arianism was wrong but not to impose any doctrinal test. This resulted in the formation of two groups: the 'subscribers', who wanted ministers to have to subscribe to a creed, and the 'non-subscribers', who didn't. Eventually, they voted. The non-subscribers won fifty-seven to fifty-three. As one of the 'no creed but the Bible' group expressed it, 'The Bible won by four.'

The result was various divisions between the two groups. They both sent their respective advice to Exeter. However, the debate had taken too long, and the local church authorities had already excluded the suspected ministers, who had then set up their own churches.

This was a moment not so much about the doctrine of the Trinity but about how doctrinal purity was to be achieved. The result was division and a lack of clear boundary lines. Over the following years, many more ministers, especially Presbyterians, became Arian in their views. This slide continued for many years and resulted in the official founding of the Unitarian Church later in the century.

Where was Watts in all this? He was at Salters' Hall, at least for some of the meetings, but when it came to the vote he is listed as absent or not present. It appears that his illness came into play again, as he says that he was not there because of an 'afflictive providence'.[1] Watts seems to have appreciated both sides of the arguments. He didn't want to make human doctrinal statements too important, but neither did he want to allow heresy to go unchecked. He later described the divisions that had arisen as a result of these events in this way:

> One must be suspected of Arianism because he thought it needless at that time to subscribe to a certain article of the established church. The other is charged with denying the perfection of scripture because he thought such a subscription necessary at that time.

What did Watts suggest himself? He thought there was a third way:

> Which is the best way to preserve truth and peace? By subscribing to the words of scripture or human forms? I think a happy medium might be found out to secure liberty and the gospel together, by everyone's declaring his own sense of scripture in his own words at all proper times, places and occasions, and particularly to the satisfaction of all persons who have any just concern therein.

---

1   This and the following quotes are from Watts' preface to a book that was republished in light of the Salters' Hall Controversy. The book was Matthew Henry, *Disputes Reviewed* (London: Eman. Matthews, 1710).

In other words, everyone should write their own statement of belief, and anyone who has any concern, such as their church, should be able to read and consider such a statement. Today this issue continues in some circles. Some groups ask people to sign a doctrinal statement so that they can be sure of what that person believes. This can be for speakers at events, prospective candidates for church positions or churches working together. Sometimes the response is made: 'I don't want to sign up to any man-made statement; I simply believe the Bible'. We can't let the 'no creed but Bible' line overrule all other considerations, though. That can too easily become a cover for not believing all of what the Bible clearly teaches. The lesson from the eighteenth century is that when this path is followed, people may soon start denying core truths of the Bible.

There is, then, an important place for doctrinal statements. What is crucial is what we put in them: they should not be so detailed as to speak about areas of legitimate difference between Christians. But on some issues it might be best to follow Watts' suggestion – to ask a minister to write his position on a topic for himself so that people can consider it and decide for themselves how it fits with what the Bible says.

Defending the Trinity

The controversy described above prompted Watts into writing on the topic of the Trinity. In 1722, he published *The Christian Doctrine of the Trinity*. The subtitle explains the content well:

> Father, Son and Spirit, three Persons and one God, asserted and proved, with their Divine Rights and Honours vindicated by plain Evidence of Scripture, without the Aid or Incumbrance of Human Schemes.

Notice the two key elements in his subtitle: there is the defence of the traditional doctrine of the Trinity but also the avoidance of 'human schemes', that is doctrinal statements and explanations of the Trinity that go far afield from the words of Scripture.

Watts begins this book referring to the Salters' Hall Controversy, which has raised this as an issue. He has, he says, examined the arguments of the Arians carefully, wondering if they have something to offer. But, he concludes, nothing has moved him from seeing Scripture as teaching the full deity of the Son and Spirit:

> The expressions of Scripture on that topic were so numerous, so evident, so firm and strong, that I could not with any justice and reason enter into the sentiments of this new scheme. But after a due survey of it, I was fully convinced, that the professors of it, who denied the Son and Spirit to have true and eternal godhead belonging to them, were so far departed from the Christian faith.[2]

However, Watts also says that he has decided that some of the traditional explanations of the Trinity go too far. They assume that they can explain what is actually a mystery. So Watts says:

> Thus while my faith grew bolder in this sacred article, my assurance as to the modes of explanation consciously abated... I began to think we had been too bold in our determinations of the 'modus' of this mystery.[3]

This means that Watts goes on in the book to defend the Trinity but avoids using schemes and explanations that traditionally would have been accepted. The result is a book which covers the Biblical material on the Trinity helpfully and convincingly, but which also says we shouldn't try to explain it too neatly.

If only he had left it there.

Unfortunately, Watts couldn't leave it there. We saw in the last chapter how Watts wanted to defend the faith as reasonable, which led him to try to explain Christian doctrine on the basis of reason. He had said that there were some doctrines we couldn't comprehend properly and that we should still accept them. The Trinity was one of those.

---

2   Watts, *Works*, 'Trinity', Volume 6, p. 415.

3   Ibid.

The problem, though, was that Watts couldn't live with his own system. He continually wanted to explain all the doctrines of the Christian faith, including the Trinity and the incarnation, so that they were clear and reasonable! He wanted to do so with good motivation: he wanted to clear the gospel of charges of irrationalism. He thought this was vital for believers to be reassured in their faith and for unbelievers to come to faith.

He also responded to ongoing publications on the topic. In his first work, *The Christian Doctrine of the Trinity*, he had made the following comment: 'I think the plain and express Scriptures sufficiently distinguish three personal agents – a Turk or an Indian that reads them without prejudice, would certainly understand most of them so.' This comment was taken up in a book responding directly to Watts (resulting in one of the most curious book titles in theological publishing):

> A Sober Appeal to a Turk or an Indian, concerning the plain sense of Scripture relating to the Trinity, being an answer to Mr I. Watts' late book.

This was by Rev. Martin Tomkins, a minister who had been dismissed as pastor by his congregation for his Arian convictions. As the title suggests, his book was a direct attack on Watts' work. While Watts did not write a direct reply, his future writings show interaction with Tomkins' arguments. He also keenly felt the charge of irrationalism that people like Tomkins threw at Watts and others who held to the traditional position. Watts couldn't bear the thought of such a charge sticking and so took up his pen once more.

Explaining the Trinity
That Watts felt compelled to write further on the Trinity because of the ongoing accusation of irrationalism is made clear in one of his prefaces:

> It seems proper therefore, for some persons to endeavour to make it appear, that there is a possibility in the reason

and nature of things, for true and eternal deity to be attributed to the Father, the Son and Holy Spirit, without danger of those absurdities and inconsistencies which are pretended to arise thence.[4]

He wrote another three works in which he tried to explain his own scheme for understanding the person of Jesus and the Trinity. Watts said his scheme was useful because it would vindicate the doctrine against the arguments and scoffing of the world. He said he wanted to give an explanation of the Trinity so as to 'remove all appearance of inconsistency', and to 'make this great doctrine appear consistent with reason'. But he was now doing exactly what he had said earlier we should avoid.

He also didn't do it very well. Watts continually struggled with the idea of three separate personalities who could be also called one. As a result, he kept on downplaying the distinct personhood of the Son and the Spirit. For the person of Jesus, the result was a rather unique and weird scheme where a created human soul was joined to the divine nature in eternity, resulting in the second person of the Trinity. This human soul, now joined with God, was the person who then became a man in the incarnation. One biographer quite reasonably says that Watts had a 'proneness to torture the mystery of godliness into a congruity with new schemes and explications.' While Watts never actually strays into Arianism, this ongoing desire to give rational explanation meant that he departed from traditional Trinitarian belief.

However, Watts was also concerned to submit his reason to Scripture, and hence he says concerning the Trinity:

> It is a general and excellent rule, that where two propositions are evidently true, we are not to reject either of them, because we cannot at present find the modus or manner how they are reconciled. I would be ever mindful of the weakness and narrowness of our understandings ...[5]

---

4 Ibid., 'Dissertations', Volume 6, pp. 545-6.

5 Ibid., 'Dissertations', Volume 6, p. 544.

The result is that he held his suggested scheme lightly. He later wrote an essay about the status such explanatory schemes should have, saying that they were not necessary for salvation but that they could be helpful to the church. Hence, he said, they should be proposed humbly and never enforced on anyone.

Watts certainly followed his own advice in this. He said of his own scheme that if anyone disagreed with it but still held to three persons in one Godhead, then that was fine by him. He was proposing it in order to try to be helpful rather than definitive. Unfortunately, the helpfulness was limited.

Watts' writings were not well received in many quarters, nor, in particular, by a minister called Thomas Bradbury. Watts and Bradbury had been good friends – Watts dedicated one of his poems to Bradbury and had him preach at the opening of the Bury Street Meeting House. However, Bradbury was a very different character from Watts: fiery, bombastic and given to withering sarcasm. It was Bradbury who had led the 'Subscribers' group which was narrowly defeated at Salters' Hall. Bradbury spoke publicly of what he regarded as Watts' descent into heresy, even accusing him of Socinianism. Watts responded:

> Let me entreat you to ask yourself, what degrees of passion and personal resentment may join and mingle themselves with your supposed zeal for the gospel. Jesus the searcher of hearts knows with what daily labour and study and with what constant addresses to the throne of grace, I seek to support the doctrine of his deity as well as you, and to defend it in the best manner I am capable of. And I shall tell you also that it was your urgent request among many others that engaged me so much further in this study than I at first intended. If I am fallen into mistakes, your private and friendly notice had done much more toward correction of them than public reproaches.[6]

Bradbury replied, saying that Watts' position was thought to be due to a personal instability and a love of his own inventions. Watts replied:

---

6   Milner, *Watts*, p. 393.

> ... as for my attempts to maintain the new and essential deity of Jesus Christ and the Holy Spirit, I have often examined my own heart, and am not conscious to myself, that pride and fondness of novelty has led me into any particular train of thoughts. ... My only aim has been to guard this doctrine against the objections and cavils of men, and to set it in the most defensible light.[7]

We see Watts here both defending himself and repeating his reason for writing in the first place.

Watts wrote various other works later in life on this same topic. His overall position, though, had not changed. In one of his later works, *The Glory of Christ as God-Man Displayed* (1746), he again repeated his expectation that his scheme would satisfy the intellectual challenge for believers and rebut the accusations of those outside the church:

> How happily will it make the whole scheme of our religion, and the book of God which reveals it, more intelligible and delightful to all those who love Christianity? And it will render this sacred volume much more defensible against the men who doubt or deny the blessed doctrines in it.[8]

He also attempted to show that his scheme, or at least part of it, was not unique to him, but rather had been held by others before him. To that end, he attached an appendix giving an abridgement of one of the works of Thomas Goodwin, a Puritan writer from the previous century. Watts maintains that he has not ventured to put forward his scheme without 'honourable precedent'. He also hopes that, given that he is in such good company, even if he is wrong, the censure he will receive from others will be 'light and gentle'. That was hoping too much. While his friends and supporters were gentle in their responses, there continued to be strong criticism of Watts.

Watts continued to wrestle with the formulation of the Trinity for the rest of his life – he could never reach

---

7 Ibid.
8 Watts, *Works*, 'The Glory of Christ', Volume 6, p. 803.

a settled position. His final comment on the matter contains a plaintive plea for understanding:

> How shall a poor weak creature be able to adjust and reconcile these clashing ideas, and to understand this mystery? Or must I believe and act blindfold, without understanding?[9]

After his death, some people tried to claim that Watts had become completely Unitarian in his views. The issues involved are complicated: some claim that he lost his faculties in his last days and didn't know what he was saying; others deny this. There are also contradictions over what was actually said and whether some writings were destroyed or not. In spite of this debate, there is no good reason to think he ever was Unitarian. Certainly his writings, while proposing an odd scheme, give no ground for such claims. What we should note, though, is that Watts' speculations here were not motivated by a desire for saying something original, making a name for himself, or a love of theological dispute. Rather his desire, however misguided in practice, was to defend the faith.

Debating deists

The Trinity wasn't the only area where Watts was trying to defend the faith. One of his main target groups throughout his life was known as the 'deists'. Once again the role of reason was at the centre of the discussion: deists believed that we could know everything we needed to know through use of reason and observation of the natural world. As a result, there was no actual need for revelation from God. Many of them thought that the Bible was God's revelation but that it only contained a 'republication' of what we could know through our reason anyway. Others questioned whether the Bible was revelation from God at all.

The deists' position then challenged how we know truth. They also challenged notions of what truth is. The focus on reason went hand in hand with a redefinition

9   Ibid., 'Remnants of Time', Volume 4, pp. 640-41.

of religion as being primarily about morality. According to their point of view, God existed, and so did some sort of afterlife, but what God wanted from us now was to be good. Most deists believed in Jesus but saw Him as only a good example and moral teacher. Some claimed that this was 'pure' Christianity, and that doctrines about sin and salvation, the Trinity and the incarnation, were later additions which corrupted the original.

The deists' book titles tell their own story. In 1696, John Toland published a book called *Christianity Not Mysterious*. He denied that the Bible was divine revelation and held up the total authority of reason. The subtitle of his work says: 'showing that there is nothing in the gospel contrary to reason, nor above it: and that no Christian doctrine can properly be called a mystery'. In other words, if our reason can't discover it and understand it, it can't be true.

Later on, in 1730, Matthew Tindal published a book called *Christianity as Old as Creation*. He believed in revelation through Jesus and the Bible, but he thought that 'natural' religion, deduced from our reason, and 'revealed' religion, originating in God, only differed in their modes of communication. The content of both was identical. Again, we can see this idea in the extended title: 'the Gospel a Republication of the Religion of Nature'. This book became known as the 'bible' of deism.

Watts knew that deism was proving attractive to many in the church. In the new rational and scientific age, it was a halfway house between traditional Christianity and outright scepticism. You could still talk about believing in God and the importance of Christian morality, but you weren't embarrassed about old-fashioned doctrine. This is the same sort of appeal that modern liberalism was to have centuries later.

Watts wrote a book in 1729 specifically to warn Christians about the dangers of deism. It was called *A Caveat Against Infidelity*. To us that title makes it sound like it was 'a mild caution against adultery'! What it actually meant in Watts' day was: 'a warning against apostasy'. His chief aim, he said, was to 'attempt a recovery of some of these doubting Christians, or to stop them in their course towards apostasy...'.[10]

He argued about the reality and effect of sin and the need for salvation by God rather than our own attempts at morality:

> By nature we are enemies to God and goodness; our own reasoning, our moral motives, our rules of philosophy, and all our self-invented methods of austere penance of mortification, will not wean our hearts from the love of sin and vanity, and work that supreme love to God in our souls, and that delight in him above all things, which is necessary in order to true happiness.[11]

He also focused on the authority of the Bible:

> No pretences to the light of reason, no vain fancies of new revelations, no devices of our own heart must dare to oppose, or contradict the rules given us in this holy book; if we reject the gospel there is nothing will serve us instead of it.[12]

At the end of the book, Watts paints a dramatic picture of two people on their deathbeds – a deist and a true Christian. The deist realizes he has no confidence before God, no certainty of mercy and no hope of eternal life. The Christian has all these things and has resulting joy and delight!

Following Tindal's book in 1730, Watts published *The Strength and Weakness of Human Reason* (1731), which we mentioned in the last chapter. This covered the whole area of what reason could and could not tell us, but it was focused directly on the deists and was a rebuttal of Tindal. Watts wrote the whole book in an interesting style: it was a conversation between three people – a deist, an orthodox minister and a mutual friend acting as moderator between them. The deist, of course, is suitably challenged

---

10   Ibid., 'Caveat', Volume 2, p. 471.
11   Ibid., 'Caveat', Volume 2, p. 474.
12   Ibid., 'Caveat', Volume 2, p. 475.

and comes to realize how inadequate his views are. This 'dialogue' style echoes the way Tindal wrote his famous work.

Deism continued to be a force against true Christianity, and Watts published two additional works which focused on the content of what they were teaching, rather than their basis in reason. The first of these was *The Redeemer and the Sanctifier* (1736). It was expressly addressed to deists in their denying the need for Jesus (the Redeemer) and the Holy Spirit (the Sanctifier). He said that he was grieved to see a 'new sort of Christianity published and propagated in the world, as leaves out the propitiatory sacrifice of our blessed saviour, and the sanctifying influences of the Holy Spirit'.[13]

Watts happily agreed with deists that we could know something of God from our reason – he believed 'natural religion' existed. But he also insisted that it could not tell us about our salvation. Natural religion would tell us only that we should be good, and we need far more than that. Watts says:

> To me it is as evident as the sun-beams, that while the New Testament restores natural religion to us in the brightest and fairest light, and lays the strongest obligations on us to perform all the duties of it; yet it still supposes the impossibility of our salvation thereby, through our own incapacity to perform these duties perfectly; and therefore it sets forth to our view the blessed sacrifice of the Son of God, which is the only true and proper atonement for our sins.[14]

He asks a series of questions: what is the meaning of the language of sacrifice applied to Jesus in the New Testament? Why is the gospel now spoken of as a mystery revealed? Why is the gospel seen as foolishness to the wise? Why did Jesus need to die? In these and other sections, Watts powerfully dissects deism and shows that it has nothing to do with New Testament religion.

---

13 Ibid., 'Redeemer and Sanctifier', Volume 3, p. 731.

14 Ibid., 'Redeemer and Sanctifier', Volume 3, p. 741.

The second work, called *Ruin and Recovery* (which we mentioned in the last chapter), came four years later, in 1740. Here Watts argued that original sin and atonement through Jesus are upheld by the principles of reason. He said that if he achieved his purpose in the book:

> The deist will have no longer any cause to triumph in the assurance of his attacks against Scripture, nor shall the Christian want matter for his satisfaction and joy, when he sees his divine religion vindicated by the powers of reason.[15]

Lessons for today

What should we learn from this?

Watts' desire to defend the faith to his generation was wonderful. His awareness of the chinks in the armour of the faith that caused people difficulties was spot on. Watts is a good example of someone standing up for the faith in areas where it was being challenged, and doing so in a way that people could understand.

In debating the deists, he took on one of the most troubling groups of his day and answered their arguments. He both appealed to them to turn to true Christianity and appealed to Christians not to be drawn to deism. We need such theologians and pastors who can react to the arguments of the day.

On the question of the Trinity, we should also say that Watts' aim was good – he wanted to defend the truth and wanted to meet the criticisms being thrown at the gospel. The problem was that he breathed the rationalistic air of his day too deeply. Rationalists said that all discussions had to be played out on the field defined by reason. Many ministers tried playing on that field and let go of the faith in the process. Watts did not go that far, but this was still the danger he fell into. In defending the faith in any age, we must not assume the only arms to be used are those which our enemy is willing to offer us. That's much easier for us to see now than it would have been for Watts in the

---

15   Ibid., 'Ruin and Recovery', Volume 6, p. 180.

moment, and the challenge for us is to discern where we might be doing the same thing without realizing it.

5
MINISTRY TO ALL

In the last couple of chapters we've seen Watts as the philosopher and theologian who defended the faith. His regular ministry, though, was as pastor to his congregation. It has to be said that much of Watts' life as pastor was pretty uneventful. He lived with the Abney family at one of their houses inside or outside London. His health continued to fluctuate, and he was often very limited in what he could do. He preached as often as he could and published various books, some of which we have already noted in the previous chapters.

In this chapter we'll look at a few events in his ministry and especially different areas he wrote about. As I've learned more about Watts, I've been struck by his incredibly varied activities – the man who was tackling Enlightenment reason at one point was writing songs for children at another.

Watts the pastor

Watts continued caring for his congregation both in public preaching and in giving private counsel. We see some of Watts' pastoral care for his congregation in letters he wrote. These are full of care and warmth but also instruction and direction. He was a good example of 'speaking the truth in love' (Eph. 4:15). Here is an example from a letter he wrote to a lady whose husband had recently died:

Madam,

When nature has vented itself a little, and poured out
its first sorrows, it is proper then to apply the means of
consolation. The skilful surgeon will let a fresh wound
bleed a little before he binds it up, and thereby prevent
inward disorders, and make surer work in healing it up.
Your griefs have had their loose, and the floods have
almost overwhelmed you. It is time now, Madam, to stop
the current, and raise your head above the waves. It is
time to fix your thoughts on all cheerful and supporting
circumstances that attend a mournful providence.[1]

Watts goes on to list reasons for hope and confidence
within grief, and to give a reminder of God's promises of
comfort. He encourages this lady to view her husband 'in
his Father's house, in the gardens of Paradise, waiting for
your ascent hither'.

Four years later, Watts sent this lady a copy of some of
his published sermons. A few of these are specifically on
death and one includes a brief account of her husband in
his last days alive. Watts sent this note with the sermons:

Madam,

When you peruse the Sermons on Death, guard your heart
from painful impressions. I would not open the wounds
that have been made, but attempt to pour the balm of the
gospel into them. You will find something in the eleventh
discourse borrowed from the dying bed of my departed
friend and brother. It may pain you a little, but I trust it
will please you more. May all grace be with you and yours
here and hereafter.[2]

Watts also wrote to people about their theological
questions. Somebody had enquired about the effect of the
Fall on our ability to respond to the gospel and so our need
of God's grace. Watts begins by commending the man's
desire to really understand the issues:

---

1   Milner, *Watts*, p. 412.
2   Ibid., p. 444.

I take pleasure, Sir, to find your honest enquiries after truth, and that you are not willing either to put off your children, or be contented yourself, with a mere set of words, instead of clear and intelligible doctrines.

He goes on to explain his understanding of our inability to respond to the gospel by ourselves:

This impotence, though it may be called natural, or rather native, as it comes to us by nature in its present corrupted state, yet it is not a lack of natural powers, either of understanding or will, to know or choose that which is good. For if there were not natural powers sufficient for this purpose, I do not see how men could be charged as criminals in not receiving the gracious offers of the gospel. This impotence, therefore, is what our divines call a moral impotence, i.e. their mind will not learn divine things, because they shut their eyes; they will refuse the proposals of grace, they shut it out of their hearts, they have delight in sin, and dislike to Christ and his salvation; they have a rooted obstinacy of will against the methods of divine mercy, and against the holiness which is connected with happiness. And yet this moral impotence is described in Scripture by such methods as represent us 'blind', or 'dead in sin', and that we can no more change our nature, than the Ethiopian can change his skin, or the leopard his spots. And the reason for these strong expressions is because God knows this natural aversion to grace and holiness is so strong and rooted in their hearts, that they will never renounce sin and receive the salvation of Christ, without the powerful influence of the Spirit of God, even that same Spirit which can cure those who are naturally blind, or can raise the dead.[3]

We see another example of Watts as pastor in his responses to some national events. For this we need some background: in 1720 and 1721, the whole of Britain was focused on the extraordinary story of a company called the South Sea Trading Company. Through a mixture of national finance and development of world trade, it managed to become the most prestigious company of its day – without really

---

3   Ibid., pp. 512-13.

doing any trade. It had some similarities to the dot-com companies that started up in the 1990s: there was huge public interest and the feeling that fortunes were to be made.

Shares in the company rocketed skywards and people were falling over themselves to buy South Sea stock. Some people made a huge amount of money as a result. However, it was a 'bubble', and before long the bubble burst. At that point, many more people lost a lot more money. It was a national scandal and various people, including some politicians, were tried and went to prison.

Watts wrote a short poem entitled 'On the Wondrous Rise of the South-Sea Stock'. It went like this:

'Tis said, the citizens have sold
Faith, truth and trade for South-Sea gold.
'Tis false! For those that know can swear
All is not gold that glistens there.

The collapse of the South Sea Company, and a number of other similar companies, bankrupted many people. As a result, the following years saw an increase in the number of suicides, especially in London. Watts responded to this by publishing a short book called *A Defence Against the Temptation to Self-Murder* (1726). This book began life as a letter Watts wrote to someone (we don't know the person's identity) who, he knew, was tempted to suicide. Watts said that the content of that letter was 'honoured by divine grace as to save a soul from perishing'. The usefulness of his letter for that one man led him to expand it and produce a book on the topic.

Watts speaks sympathetically of the temptation to suicide and the way in which Satan will deceive people. He explains his aim in writing as follows:

It is the design of this little treatise to discover the infinite mischief of his [Satan's] temptations, and to teach mankind how they may resist and defeat his fatal purposes.[4]

---

4   This and the following quotes are from Watts, *Works*, 'Defence', Volume 2.

Watts begins the book with Biblical arguments as to why suicide is wrong. However, he knows that such an assertion is not enough and he wanted to be practically helpful to people. Hence, he goes on to deal with the reasons people give for suicide and then with steps people can take to avoid temptation. So, for example, he says:

> Love not anything in this world so much as that the loss of it would throw you quite off your guard, and make you abandon yourself to wild and extravagant methods of relief. Let your affections be so subdued and kept in such good order that the common calamities of life may not utterly confound, though they may surprise you. If you place your whole happiness in any of the attainments of this world, you expose yourself to this bloody temptation when you suffer the loss of those idols.

Watts goes on to give practical steps about remaining busy and active, avoiding spending time in the alehouse and Scriptures to memorize.

Watts knew people faced bankruptcy and poverty, and felt overwhelmed by the shame that is involved. He also knew that some people's personalities or temperaments led them to be more depressive and so more tempted. He responds to all this with both sympathy and the call to trust God.

So, Watts as a pastor was compassionate and under-standing of people and the pressures they faced. However, he gently but firmly held to God's truth and called people to live in line with it.

Watts the teacher of children

Watts was very concerned for the instruction of children. His *The Art of Reading and Writing English* (1721) was the first of a number of educational books he would write. In it, he had an unorthodox suggestion: that children should be taught in English! That sounds perfectly obvious to us, but at the start of the eighteenth century the accepted position was that all education should be in Latin. Watts wrote on the title page of his book:

Let all the foreign tongues alone
'Till you can spell and read your own.

There was another debate going on in the 1720s about education in addition to this one about the appropriate language to use. It focused on another question we would never ask today: should poor children be educated at all? Amazingly (to us), some people answered, 'No'.

Protestant charity schools had started at the end of the previous century, at least partly in response to the presence of Roman Catholic schools. The idea was both to help poor children in life by providing an education, but also to take the opportunity to teach them the gospel. Among many this provision was seen as an obvious Christian responsibility and opportunity.

Not everyone saw things that way, though. Most notably, Bernard Mandeville, a philosopher, wrote an essay against the work of charity schools in 1723. Mandeville had a number of arguments: public charity resulted in people being lazy and encouraged dependence; educating the poor gave them the idea that they could do more than menial labour, and then who would do such tasks? and education of the poor would disturb the natural balance of people's position in society. This perspective seems incredibly harsh to us but was not unusual when it was written.

Watts responded with *An Essay Towards the Encouragement of Charity Schools* (1728), which was an expansion of a sermon on the topic from the previous year. Watts engaged Mandeville's argument directly. For example, he said that to keep the poor ignorant was to make them vulnerable to being misled and to being rebellious. He accepted that there could be dangers with people aspiring to a higher station in life, but maintained that everyone deserved access to both rudimentary education and Bible teaching. While Watts wasn't the only one making these arguments at the time, in much of what he said he was well ahead of his day.

Watts the children's pastor

Watts' concern for children didn't stop at education. He also gave himself to their spiritual growth. We see this in three publications, all of which were popular, but one of which was a best-seller.

Teaching children to sing

The best-seller was *Divine Songs Attempted in Easy Language for the Use of Children* (1715). Watts says in the preface that those who teach religion to children have a great responsibility and says that this book of songs is designed to help them in it. He thinks learning religion through song has four advantages:

1. It is more enjoyable

2. It is more easily remembered

3. It gives children something to continue to think over for themselves

4. The songs can be used by families

Watts was very restricted by the tunes he had available (he didn't write music himself), so these songs look like hymns to us. However, they are hymns aimed at children in language, style and content. Watts was not the first to do this and probably was inspired by some children's poems in existence, such as those by John Bunyan. However, poetry was his great gift, and so he did it very well.

Here's part of a song entitled 'Praise to God for our Redemption':

Our father ate forbidden fruit,
And from his glory fell;
And we, his children, thus were brought
To death, and near to hell.

Blest be the Lord, that sent his Son
To take our flesh and blood!
He for our lives gave up his own,
To make our peace with God.

Watts included topics we wouldn't find among children's songs today, such as 'Praise for birth and education in a Christian land' or 'Praise to God for learning to read'. Many of them also focus on morality, such as 'Against quarrelling and fighting', or 'Obedience to parents'. The one against quarrelling and fighting goes like this:

> Let dogs delight to bark and bite,
> For God hath made them so;
> Let bears and lions growl and fight,
> For 'tis their nature too.
>
> But, children, you should never let
> Such angry passions rise;
> Your little hands were never made
> To tear each other's eyes.

The story is told of how these songs were used in the conversion of one lady. She was a single mother and one day heard her daughter repeat some of her own terrible language. Her religious background meant that she was worried that she was heading to hell herself and leading her daughter there by her example. She had some memory of Watts' songs for children and so immediately bought a copy to be able to use them to teach her daughter. Opening the book, she read:

> Just as the tree cut down, that falls
> To north or southward, there it lies:
> So man departs to heaven or hell,
> Fixed in the state wherein he dies.

She kept reading and was led to faith in Jesus.

The popularity and influence of these children's songs were incredible. Judged by the number of editions, this was the best-selling children's book of all time – there were over six hundred editions, resulting in approximately seven million copies being sold. There were also numerous imitations that followed in Watts' wake over the following hundred years or so. Lewis Carroll later parodied some of Watts' poems. Watts had written:

How doth the little *busy bee,* improve each shining hour.

This inspired Carroll to write:

How doth the little crocodile, improve his shining tail.

One author says of these songs: 'In verse technique and in understanding of the child's world, *Divine Songs* was unprecedented and unrivalled.'[5]

Teaching children to pray

Watts also taught children to pray. In 1728, he published *Prayers Composed for the Use and Imitation of Children.* This was a remarkable work. Watts wanted to help children pray but he knew that, as with his songs, he had to write at their level. So, as the subtitle of his book says, his prayers were 'suited to their different ages and their various occasions'.

As this subtitle suggests, Watts wrote a variety of prayers both for different ages of children and for different occasions in their lives. For Watts, the understanding of children in prayer was crucial. He hated the thought that children would be taught to say words which were only words to them. Mindless repetition would only teach children that prayer involved *saying* something rather than *meaning* something! He explains:

> I am well satisfied that the best way of teaching children, both in matters divine and human, is to lead them into some tolerable idea and conception of all the things signified by the words they are taught to use, as soon as those words are taught them; that they may not be accustomed, even in their younger days, to deal in mere sounds, to talk without ideas, and to speak words and syllables without a meaning.[6]

In light of this principle, Watts adapted the language and length of prayer for four different age groups, from young children of only three or four years old up to teenagers. He also worked very hard at the language he used, which, he

---

5   Davis, *Watts*, p. 84.
6   Watts, *Works*, 'Prayers for Children', Volume 3, p. 498.

says, 'cost him much labour'. He wanted to avoid religious and complicated language which children wouldn't understand, but still express the great truths of the gospel. This is where Watts was a master: finding the right words that captured the truth he wanted in simple language, but without becoming simplistic or dull.

So, for infants, he wrote these:

> For the morning: Save me, O Lord, from evil all this day long, and let me love and serve thee forever.

> For the evening: I pray thee, O Lord, forgive me whatsoever I have done amiss this day, and keep me safe all this night.

For an older child, the evening prayer became this:

> O Lord our heavenly Father, thou hast made the night for us to take our rest. I pray thee, look down upon me, and watch over me while I sleep; for if thou take care of me, I need be afraid of nothing.

> Accept the thanks of a child, for all the good things I have this day received; and as I lie down in peace, this evening, so let me awake and rise again in peace, in the morning, to serve thee.

> Thou seest and hearest everything, that I have said or done all this day: O pardon every one of my faults, and be not angry with me, for thy son Jesus Christ has suffered death for our sins, and I desire to trust in him to save me from thy anger.

> Let me learn to know thee, while I am a child, and begin to fear thee, and love thee, and to do thy will with delight; and I humbly ask that thy Holy Spirit may instruct and assist me, in all things needful for me to know and to do.

> Help me to honour my father and mother, to obey all my teachers and governors, to love my brothers and sisters, my friends and neighbours, as I would have them love me. Let me not be an enemy to any person whatsoever, and suffer not others to be enemies to me.

I entreat thee, O Lord, for Christ's sake, give me everything that is best both for my soul and body, for thou are wise and gracious, and able to do better things for me than I am able to ask.

And when I have served thee, to my utmost, in this world, then take my soul to live with thee in heaven, where I shall serve thee far better than I can do on earth, and give thee glory, for ever and ever. Amen.

That this is what Watts expected of an eight-year-old perhaps shows that expectations were higher back then than today!

The variety of occasions that Watts includes shows something of the age in which he lived. He includes prayers for recovery from sickness; on the loss of a parent; at the birth of a sibling; after a grievous sin; for children of rich, poor and middling parents; enquiring after a trade or profession; and on receiving new clothes! What impressed me most on reading them is the thoughtfulness with which every aspect of life is brought under God's rule and looked at with the eye of Scripture.

Teaching children the gospel

The last of Watts' books for children were his catechisms. Catechisms are a way of learning the truth of the gospel and the Christian life using questions and answers. The idea is that the person learns the answers by heart. Watts had been taught this way by his father. There were many catechisms in existence, the most famous of which was the *Westminster Catechism* from the previous century. This was (and is) a marvellous summary of the Christian faith. It came in two forms – a longer and a shorter catechism. The idea of the shorter version was that it was suitable for younger people to learn. Watts, however, felt that it was still too long and complicated for children, and a brief glance at it will convince most people that he was right. In fact, others, such as John Owen, had previously recognized this and written simpler catechisms for children. Watts' concern was again that children don't simply learn a set of words that they can repeat but can understand what they are saying.

So, as with songs and prayers, Watts wanted a catechism designed specifically for children. And, as with his prayers, he wrote different versions for different ages. It was called *Catechisms, or Instructions in the Principles of the Christian Religion, and the History of Scripture, composed for Children and Youth, according to their different ages*, and was published in 1730. He had no desire to replace the Westminster catechisms, but only to provide simpler versions, until people were old enough to read the longer ones.

Once again, Watts refers to what hard work it is to try to render the great truths of the gospel in simple language:

> What laborious diligence has been used to seek out the plainest and most familiar forms of speech, that the great things of God and the mysteries of the gospel might be brought down to the capacities of children.[7]

Here is a section from the catechism for three-to-six-year-olds:

Q: Do you know who Jesus Christ is?

A: He is God's own son, who came down from heaven to save us from our sins, and from God's anger.

Q: What has Christ done toward the saving of men?

A: He obeyed the law of God himself, and has taught us to obey it also.

Q: And what has Christ suffered in order to save men?

A: He died for sinners who have broken the law of God, and deserved to die themselves.

Q: Where is Jesus Christ now?

A: He is alive again, and gone to heaven to provide a place there for all that serve God and love his son Jesus.

---

7   Ibid., 'Catechisms', Volume 3, p. 203.

Q: Can you of yourself love and serve God and Christ?

A: No, I cannot do it of myself, but God will help me by his own Spirit if I ask him for it.

Again, this is far above what we might expect of a young child today, but was significantly simpler compared to any other catechisms available. Charles Spurgeon, the famous nineteenth-century minister, commented:

> Dr Watts' Catechism, which I learned myself, is so simple, so interesting, so suggestive, that a better condensation of Scriptural knowledge will never be written; and the marvel is that such a little miracle of instruction should have been laid aside by teachers.

In all his writing for children, Watts knew that many people thought he was wasting his time. He referred to those who thought his time was 'employed in too mean a service while I write for babes'. He replied:

> I content myself with this thought: that nothing is too mean for a servant of Christ to engage in, if he can thereby most effectually promote the kingdom of his blessed master. If the God whom I serve will bless my labours to sow the seeds of religion in the understanding and hearts of children, I shall hope there will arise a fair harvest of the fruits of holiness in the succeeding generation, and some revenue of glory to my creator and redeemer.[8]

In his attention to the importance of children and his age-appropriate content for them, Watts was well ahead of his time.

Watts the educator

Watts also wrote educational works for adults. We've mentioned one of these already – his book *Logic*. Watts followed this up with a more practical volume called *The Improvement of the Mind* (1741). This was all about how to think well – it was logic practically applied.

---

8   Ibid., 'Catechisms', Volume 3, pp. 202-3.

Watts wanted to persuade people of the need to think well and then to help them do so. He said:

> A well-furnished library, and a capacious memory, are indeed of singular use toward the improvement of the mind. But if all your learning be nothing else but a mere amassment of what others have written, without a due penetration into the meaning, and without a judicious choice and determination of your own sentiments, I do not see what title your head has to true learning above your shelves.[9]

This is something I've learnt from Watts: true learning is not simply about knowing facts and what other people have said; it's about using our own minds well to come to our own convictions. Watts encouraged people not to hold to an opinion until they had a foundation for it in their own minds. He spoke of the need for humility such that we could admit error and so progress in true knowledge. He told people to listen to both sides of an argument, rather than being easily persuaded by just one side.

One of Watts' sections was on 'How to read a book'. You might respond thinking, 'What's the point of that?' Watts had a good point, though. He felt that people didn't know how to read properly – that is, they didn't know how to *think* while they were reading. Here's part of what he says:

> Where the author is obscure, enlighten him; where he is imperfect, supply his deficiencies; where he is too brief and concise, amplify a little, and set his notions in fairer view; where he is redundant, mark those paragraphs to be retrenched; when he trifles and grows impertinent, abandon those passages or pages; where he argues, observe whether his reasons be conclusive; if the conclusion be true, and yet the arguments weak, endeavour to confirm it by better proofs; where he derives or infers any propositions darkly or doubtfully, make the justice of the inference appear, and add further inferences or corollaries, if such occur to your mind; where you suppose he is in a mistake, propose your objections and correct his sentiments; what

---

9   Ibid., 'Improvement of the Mind', Volume 5, p. 198.

he writes so well as to approve itself to your judgement both as just and useful, treasure it up in your memory and count it as part of your intellectual gains.[10]

I think it's fair to say that few of us read a book with such rigour! Watts' *Improvement of the Mind* was well received and widely used. Dr Samuel Johnson, who is famous for his dictionary, thought very highly of this book. In fact, he said:

Few books have been perused by me with greater pleasure than his *Improvement of the Mind*, ... Whoever has the care of instructing others may be charged with deficiency in his duty if this work is not recommended.[11]

Dr Johnson's respect for Watts in this and other books can also be seen in his famous *Dictionary*. Unlike modern dictionaries, Johnson's work quotes what other writers have said about the meaning of words, and Watts is quoted hundreds of times.

One of Watts' most repeated themes in education is from the philosopher John Locke. Locke spoke of the need for 'clear and distinct ideas'. What he meant was that, when we speak about a topic, the first thing we must do is be precise and clear on what it is we are speaking about and what we are saying about it. Watts agreed fully:

The first rule is this, seek after a clear and distinct conception of things as they are in their own nature, and do not content yourselves with obscure and confused ideas, where clearer are to be attained.[12]

One of Watts' concerns was that in theology people used words without being clear. As a result, they bred confusion or covered over lack of understanding. In discussing debates in theology, Watts says great advantages would come if only we were clear about what we meant:

10   Ibid., 'Improvement of the Mind', Volume 5, pp. 207-8.
11   Samuel Johnson, *Works* (Troy, N.Y.: Pafraets Book Co., 1903), Volume 11, p. 48.
12   Watts, *Works*, 'Logic', Volume 5, p. 41.

If we could but always confine every term to one certain determinate idea, we should gain and preserve much clearer ideas of things; we should make swifter and larger advances in knowledge; we should cut off a thousand occasions for mistake, and take away a multitude of controversies.[13]

Watts applied this principle to teaching children as well, saying that unless we explain clearly what we mean there will be disastrous results:

... they will get into a habit of dealing in sounds instead of ideas, and of mistaking words for things, than which there is scarcely any thing more pernicious to the reason and understanding of a man; nor is there anything that tends more to corrupt and spoil the judgement in its early exercises.[14]

Watts wrote on other topics too. There was a work on astronomy which, like many other books, Watts wrote because he felt there was no suitable textbook currently available. Watts was not trying to break new ground in this, but simply to present existing knowledge, and to do so in an easily accessible way. This is seen in the recommendation of his book by a leading scientist, who spoke of the 'perspicuity of thought and ease of expression' which ran through Watts' writing.

Watts also wrote on philosophical matters. The philosophy of the day debated topics such as innate ideas, space and matter, whether the soul is always thinking, and the nature of personal identity. Watts was by no means a leading voice in these areas, but he was an excellent analyst. He opened up these topics and made careful and helpful arguments as to which side was right. For him, study was also to be an aid to faith; he always looked to find a lesson in humility or awe of God, rather than simply discovering bare truth. As Dr Johnson commented:

Whatever he took in hand was, by his incessant solicitude for souls, converted to theology. As piety predominated in

13   Ibid., 'Freedom of Will', Volume 6, p. 379.
14   Ibid., 'Catechisms', Volume 3, p. 217.

his mind, it is diffused over his works. ... it is difficult to read a page without learning, or at least wishing, to be better. The attention is caught by indirect instruction, and he that sat down only to reason, is on a sudden compelled to pray.[15]

I know what Johnson means – I've experienced exactly that in reading Watts' works!

Recognition of his contribution to education and to theology came in 1728 when the Universities of both Edinburgh and Aberdeen bestowed on him a Doctor of Divinity. From then on he was 'Dr Watts'.

Watts the adviser

Watts was also looked to as a leader and often gave advice and encouragement to younger ministers. One friend of his was in ministry in Southampton at Watts' family's old church. This friend, Henry Francis, was discouraged in his work and was considering leaving the church. Watts wrote to him:

Your last is now before me with all the long detail of discouragements which you enumerate there. I accept many of them to be true, and the future prospects of the dissenting interest in Southampton, after the lives of some few persons, is somewhat unpleasing and afflictive, if we look merely to appearances. But I have a few things to offer which will in some measure, I hope, reconcile your thoughts to a long continuance among them:

1. Consider what great things God has done for the dissenting interest in Southampton by your means...

2. There are some persons in whom God has begun a good work by your means. Oh do not think of forsaking them!

3. There is scarcely any people in England who love their minister and honour and esteem him more than your do you...

4. Where is the man who is better qualified for carrying on God's work in the town than you are?

---

15   Johnson, *Works*, Volume 3, p. 668.

5. If you leave, where will you go? The situation is the same in many places as it is with you and much worse.

6. Consider whether this be not a temptation thrown in your way to discourage you in your work.

7. Let us remember that we are not engaged in a work that depends on reasonings and prospects and probabilities and present appearances, but upon the hand and Spirit of God. If he will work, who shall hinder?

Farewell dear brother: meditate on these things. Turn your thoughts to the objects which are more joyful, and the occasions you have for thankfulness. Praise and thanksgiving are springs to the soul and give it new activity.[16]

Henry Francis decided to stay in Southampton.

In his position as a theologian and an educator, Watts became influential in the education of ministers, especially within his denomination, the Congregationalists. He was on the board of two important organizations which oversaw theological education. This meant responsibility for selection of tutors and students, finance for training, and general supervision of the dissenting academies.

He was also often asked for advice on a curriculum or on recommendations for suitable tutors. One example was the curriculum at an academy near Leicester with the new tutor Philip Doddridge. Doddridge was an admirer of Watts:

I have received so much entertainment and advantage from his writings, that I cannot but have an affection for his person, and should consider myself happy if providence should ever give me an opportunity of cultivating an acquaintance with him.[17]

Discussion of the academy's course gave such an opportunity, and Watts was to become something of a mentor to Doddridge.

---

16   Fountain, *Watts*, pp. 81-2.

17   Milner, *Watts*, p. 433.

Watts' involvement in selecting students for training for ministry led him to write an interesting work called *Questions Proper for Students in Divinity, Candidates of the Ministry, and Young Christians* (1740). This is simply a series of questions which the student should ask themselves. It pushes students to examine their own hearts – their motives and desires – and so to be aware of how they need to grow in themselves, as well as in knowledge.

The very first questions are these:

What was my great design, in devoting myself to study for the ministry, and what is my daily view and purpose in pursuing it?

Have I entirely given up myself to our Lord Jesus Christ, as a Christian, that I may be fitter to become a faithful minister?

Do I every day seek direction and blessing from God, in all my studies for this end?

Later questions ask about areas of theology or about practical ministry. Examples of the second group include:

How would you convince a sober man that he has no sufficient righteousness of his own to justify him before God, by reason and by Scripture?

How would you present Christ as answering all the needs of perishing sinners?

In what manner would you direct persons who complain of the power and prevalence of special sins or temptations?

How would you comfort serious Christians under darkness who fear God is departed from them?

Later questions are directed to young ministers about their work of ministry. For example:

Do I resolve, through the aids of divine grace, to be 'faithful to him who hath put me into the ministry', and to 'take heed to the ministry which I have received in the Lord, that I may fulfil it'? (1 Tim. 1:12, Col. 4:17).

Do I preach to the people 'not myself but Jesus Christ the Lord, and myself as their servant for Jesus' sake'? (2 Cor. 4:5).

Do I 'watch over the souls of men as one that must give an account, being solicitous that I may do it with joy and not with grief'? (Heb. 13:17).

Further questions ask about faithfulness, prayer, humility, perseverance and more. As someone who has been a student training for ministry and then worked as a pastor, I can say how penetrating and wise Watts' questions are. They are written by someone who knows the Bible, knows pastoral ministry and knows people's hearts.

What then have we seen? In Watts' middle years of ministry, he was handicapped by poor health but was still amazingly productive. We see his heartfelt care for his congregation. We see his incredibly wide range of abilities and knowledge. We see his concern for children. We see perhaps above all that in each area, whomever he is speaking to or writing for, his desire is to be a blessing to them. That desire shows itself in very practical ways – he writes in a way that is understandable and clear; he writes for children, not about them; he brings skills and knowledge within people's reach; and he is happy to write a book simply of questions in the hope that it will be useful to students and ministers. He was a man who ministered to all.

6
PROMOTING THE HEART

Standing against 'cool' religion

In an earlier chapter we were introduced to the eighteenth-century 'enthusiast'. Enthusiasts claimed they had a hot-line to heaven and spoke about their ecstatic experiences of God. Enthusiasts were taken to be a bit mad, even very mad. People said such things came from being 'melancholy' (being a bit depressive) or having an 'overheated imagination' (being a bit unstable). No one wanted to be called an enthusiast! We've also seen how everyone wanted to be considered 'reasonable'. Being rational and intellectual meant you were respected. It was the very opposite of enthusiasm.

This resulted in Christianity being very 'cool'. The focus was on knowledge, not feelings. The main aim was to reform how people lived, not what they experienced. Any talk of how you felt about God, or of your experience of God, was ruled out. Talk like that and you might be called an 'enthusiast', and that wasn't being 'reasonable'.

Isaac Watts had a problem with this cool, reasonable religion. He believed that true Christianity involved more than right knowledge; it involved our hearts. He pointed to what Jesus said was the greatest commandment: to love God with all our heart, soul, mind and strength (Mark 12:30). Such love, argued Watts, must involve our feelings for God (or, as they were called back then, our 'passions' or 'affections').

Also, said Watts, God has made us to experience and to feel, so why shouldn't we experience Him? We should feel love for God and we should experience His love for us. He argued:

> Has he formed my soul to delight and love and has he confined these sweet and pleasurable capacities only to be employed about creatures, when the Creator himself is supreme in loveliness? Will not this most amiable of beings expect that I should love himself, and give me leave to make him my delight?[1]

Watts knew that many people in his day had made religion all about right and reasonable doctrines, but, he said, this has led to an external, hypocritical faith. People might be very knowledgeable, they might be very moral, and they might be very religious, but none of that is the real thing. Here's how he put it:

> It is not enough for the eye to be lifted up to him, or the knee to bow before him; it is not enough for the tongue to speak of him, or the hand to act for his interest in the world; all this may be done by painted hypocrites whose religion is all disguise and vanity. But the heart with all the inward powers and passions must be devoted to him in the first place: This is religion indeed. The great God values not the service of men, if the heart not be in it.[2]

So one of Watts' great aims was to promote heart religion: to tell people that true religion must involve their hearts. To tell Christians who did feel love for God that that was OK, that it wasn't being mad; in fact, it was good and right. He said he wanted to 'vindicate the passionate believer'.

But Watts also thought that there *were* people who were a bit mad! He thought 'enthusiasm' in its bad sense existed and that it wasn't a good thing. He said:

> On the other hand, it must be acknowledged also, there have been many persons who have made their religion consist too much in the working of their passions, without a due exercise of reason in the things of God.

---

1 Watts, *Works*, 'Love of God', Volume 2, p. 697.

2 Ibid., 'Love of God', Volume 2, p. 640.

They have contented themselves with some divine raptures without seeking after clear conceptions of divine things, or building their faith and hope, and practice, upon a just and solid foundation of sacred knowledge.[3]

These people, said Watts, made their relationship with God *all* about their feelings. They have no foundation of understanding because they haven't tried to use their minds to grow in knowledge. They've been happy just 'experiencing' God. But there are great dangers down that road.

So, Watts wanted to promote true, vital Christianity involving experience of God and feeling something about God. But he also wanted to guard against emotionalism and warn people away from the dangers of subjective impressions and experiences.

This led him to write two linked works. The first was a general work on the 'passions' or, as we would say, the emotions. But it was the second work which really got into the issue. The title reveals its subject matter:

Discourses of the Love of God and Its Influence on all the Passions: With a Discovery of the Right Use and Abuse of Them in Matters of Religion

Let's take a look at what he said and what we can learn about the need for heart religion today.

How the heart works

Watts defined the passions as the response we feel because of the characteristics of an object or a situation. For instance, if an object is unusual, we feel surprise; if it is beautiful, we feel desire; if it is dangerous, we feel fear. Passions are what we feel when we see, hear about, remember or anticipate an object or situation.

So passions, or emotions, come from our perceptions, but they result in feeling something in our body. Watts thought there was such a close relationship between our mind and body that what we regard in our mind, we will feel in our body, at least to some extent. In fact, he said that

---

3   Ibid., 'Love of God', Volume 2, pp. 637-8.

if we believed something but didn't feel anything about it, he doubted whether we truly believed it.

Watts thought there were 'primary passions' of love and hate, and that the other passions flowed from those. So, for example, if we love something and we don't have it, we feel longing; if we gain something we love, we feel joy; if we have something we love but then lose it, we feel sadness; and so on. The same is true for the things we hate. If we are faced with the possibility of something we hate, we feel trepidation; if we avoid something we hate, we feel relief; if we experience something we hate, we feel sadness. That analysis isn't unique to Watts; it has a long history among people who've thought about such things.

It's a helpful analysis, though. It means that for whatever we feel we can ask the question: what love or what hate is producing this feeling? It means that behind all that we feel is ultimately the love of our hearts. That's going to be important in Watts' arguments later on.

What are the emotions for?

Watts thought you could divide up a person into roughly three bits: we have a mind, we have emotions, and we have a will. We are thinking, feeling and acting people. Each of these areas has a different role in how we are to live. Reason should evaluate and come to correct views on what is right and wrong, true and false. The will should then choose in accordance with reason.

But what about feelings? What are they for? There are two answers. First, they allow us to experience enjoyment; they are for our pleasure. If all we had was reason and will, we would know and act but we would be more like machines than people. Our passions mean we can experience pleasure, happiness, contentment and more in our lives.

But secondly, the passions form a link between the reason and will in providing motivation:

> Consider, my friends, what were the passions made for? Not merely for the conscious pleasure of human nature, but to give it vigour and power for useful actions.[4]

---

4   Ibid., 'Love of God', Volume 2, p. 689.

How we feel about something animates us to pursue it or avoid it. Watts draws a contrast with our reason here. Our reason may tell us that something is good or bad, right or wrong, but reason doesn't motivate us. It when we *feel* that something is good and we love it that we pursue it actively, and when we *feel* that something is evil and fear it that we really try to avoid it. Hence Watts refers to the passions as the 'engine' which drives us.

Emotions: created, fallen, restored

Watts thought that God created people with passions which were meant to be guided by their reason and motivate their will. Talking about Adam before his fall into sin, Watts said:

> Reason gave the lead; affection and will gladly followed. His natural powers had no uneasy contest, there was no civil war nor rebellion amongst them to interrupt his happiness.[5]

Watts' understanding of how we are to work is that the reason understands, the emotions are inclined and the will chooses accordingly. When everything works in harmony like that, then it is all wonderful. As he says above, there's no 'civil war' going on inside us.

But then comes sin. Sin results in exactly such an internal civil war. Sin means we fix our passions on 'improper objects', that is, we love what we shouldn't. Or, we fix our passions on the right objects but with 'excessive degree', that is, we love them too much. As we saw earlier, for Watts, the disorder of our passions lies at the heart of sin in our lives.

This means that our reason is 'opposed and beclouded' and it loses its clearness of judgment. For Watts, sin means the passions rebel against the mind and overpower it. We are reminded here of Watts' tendency to think of sin operating in our passions, but not in our minds, whereas the Biblical picture involves the distortion of our thinking just as much as our feeling (see Rom. 1:21-23). But Watts

---

5   Ibid., 'Sermons', Volume 1, p. 9.

does capture well the way our hearts are involved in sin: we love wrongly now.

The motivational power of our passions means this leads to disaster. We've seen how Watts likened the passions to an 'engine' which drives us. Now, after sin, he says, they are a 'most powerful engine of mischief'. One of Watts' hymns puts it this way:

> Our hasty wills rush blindly on
> Where rising passion rolls,
> And thus we make our fetters strong
> To bind our slavish souls.[6]

In our sinfulness, we follow wherever our passions lead us and they lead us into slavery. Watts emphasizes how terrible our situation is here and how we are powerless to change it. This leads people to live more like animals than those made in the image of God:

> Ungoverned passions break all the bonds of human society of peace, and would change the tribes of mankind into brutal herds, or make the world a mere wilderness of savages. Passion unbridled would violate all the sacred ties of religion, and raise the sons of men in arms against their creator. Where passion runs riot, there are none of the rights of God or man secure from its insolences.[7]

But then comes God and His salvation. God restores and renews us so that we start to work as we were supposed to. God comes to '… reform our natures, to put all our misplaced and disjointed powers into their proper order again, and to maintain this divine harmony and peace'.[8]

Our reason is able to lead again, our passions start to love and hate as they should and our wills follow. This is the work of the Spirit in bringing new life and renewal. There is 'a great and holy change, wrought in the powers of your soul, your understanding, will and affections, by the Spirit of God'.

---

6   Ibid., 'Horae Lyricae', Volume 4, p. 370.

7   Ibid., 'Doctrine of the Passions', Volume 2, p. 581.

8   Ibid., 'Sermons', Volume 1, p. 10.

Watts pictures God saying to the sinner: 'I will heal him; that is, I will renew all his inwards passions, I will renew all his affections.' It's a lovely picture. The love of our hearts has become distorted and led our lives astray. God doesn't respond by simply telling us what is right and wrong – our minds don't just need more information. Nor does He simply hand out laws and commands – our wills don't just need more enforcement. Instead, He renews us inside – our hearts need to be healed.

Again, we see this in one of Watts' hymns:

> The Spirit, like some heav'nly wind,
> Blows on the sons of flesh,
> New-models all the carnal mind,
> And forms the man afresh.[9]

For Watts, our passions play a key role in how we were created, how we have fallen and how we are restored. This fact forms the basis for promoting heart religion: our experience of God and our love for God.

Experiencing God

True Christianity means we experience God. On that Watts is clear. He begins with conversion. Remember Watts' perspective on the close connection between our understanding and our feeling? This means that coming to faith cannot simply be an intellectual act. Watts says:

> Can the thirsty soul taste of the running water and not find refreshment, since God, who created the water, has ordained it to refresh the thirsty…? No more can a guilty, distressed and penitent sinner believe the truths of the gospel, and trust in *Jesus* the saviour, and yet find no relief.[10]

Watts argues that the gospel should have an effect on all of a person, including his or her passions. In speaking about coming to knowledge of forgiveness, he says:

---

9   Ibid., 'Sermons', Volume 1, p. 179.
10   Ibid., 'Sermons', Volume 1, p. 197.

Will it not fill the soul with overflowing gratitude, and make the lips abound in expressions of joy and praise? And will not these be attended with a peaceful and pleasing aspect, and establish a sweet serenity in the heart and eyes?

You see the picture? True knowledge of God in His goodness and His forgiveness to us should result in feeling something as well as knowing something.

Now, having said that, Watts knows that many different factors will influence how much anyone might feel. He mentions our physical health, our constitution, different nationalities (he comments on how the Scots, the Welsh and the English have their different temperaments), and even the weather (seasonal affective disorder is not a new idea). So, he's very pastorally wise in this.

He also says that a will resolved to live for God is better proof of true conversion than any sudden flash of emotion. Yet, he still says we should feel something in our new relationship with God. Conversion, forgiveness, adoption, new life by the Spirit – these all have some experiential aspect to them. In this way, Watts countered the cool, knowledge-only religion of his day, and told people it is OK to feel.

He also says that God may give particular experiences to people. This is less common, but Watts wants to make room for it. God may give people a particularly strong awareness of His love for them. This doesn't simply happen by itself; Watts says it will usually come as people are reminding themselves of God's truth, while they are praying or meditating. But God will give them a 'powerful and pleasant sense' that they belong to Him. Or, they will have an experience where they are 'raised to holy raptures, to heavenly joy and assurance'. Such things are not the effects of an 'overheated imagination'; they are, in their own way, perfectly reasonable to believe in.

Christians should even call on God for experience of His love. We see this in Watts' hymns. In one, he wrote:

Come, dear Lord, descend and dwell
By faith and love in ev'ry breast;

Then shall we know, and taste, and feel
The joys that cannot be express'd.[11]

But while Watts wanted to justify such experience of God, he didn't want people to look for such experiences as their source of assurance. He reassured people:

> Ten thousand Saints are arrived safe at Paradise, who have not been favoured, like St Paul, with a Rapture in the third Heaven, nor could ever arise to the affectionate Transports, and devout Joys of Mrs Rowe.[12]

The Mrs Rowe mentioned here was someone who had written about her experience of God (she's the lady who'd turned down Watts on his offer of marriage). Watts saw her as an example of the more unusual 'raptures' that God can give. Watts says her example is not to be laughed at, but that the majority of Christians arrive safely in heaven without ever having had such experiences.

For reassurance, Watts pointed people to their growth in godliness more than their ecstatic experiences:

> Value mortification to sin more than raptures; for mortification is a certain sign that the Spirit of God dwells in us, and that we are heirs of life.[13]

Given these cautions, you might ask why Watts was bothered to speak about experience of God at all. The reason is that he wanted to defend such experience. He thought the Bible and Christian experience taught us these things and that we should not be ashamed of them. He knew that in speaking like this, he was in danger of being called an enthusiast. But he was prepared to live with that and wasn't prepared to back off for the sake of being thought 'reasonable'. In an age that valued reason and intellect highly, Watts provided a balancing voice for Christians concerning the importance of heart religion.

---

11   Ibid., 'Hymns', Volume 4, p. 190.

12   ———, 'Preface,' in *Devout Exercises of the Heart in Meditation and Soliloquy, Prayer and Praise, by Elizabeth Singer Rowe* (London: R. Hett, 1738), p. xxv.

13   ———, *Works*, 'Evangelical Discourses', Volume 2, p. 103.

Loving God

We've seen how Watts speaks of heart religion in our experience *of* God. But there's another side to heart religion and that's what we feel *for* God – our love for Him. Watts reflects on Deuteronomy 6:5: 'Love the Lord your God with all your heart and all your mind and all your strength', encouraging passionate heartfelt love for God while fighting against the cool, reasonable faith of his day. Surely, Jesus is the most beautiful of beings and so we should truly love Him. Watts says:

> Our hearts are cold as well as dark: How seldom do we see that fervency of spirit in religious duties which God requires? How cool is our love to the greatest and best of beings? How languid and indifferent are our affections to the Son of God, the chief of ten thousand and altogether lovely? And how much does the devotion of our souls lack its proper ardour and vivacity?[14]

This leads Watts to explore what is involved in the love of God. First, he says, love for God means knowing truth about God so that we see Him rightly. Remember, our passions are raised by the properties of the object. So, says Watts:

> It is not to be expected that we should love God supremely, or with all our heart, if we have not known him to be more excellent, and more desirable, than all other things we are acquainted with. We must have the highest opinion of his transcendent worth, or we cannot love him above all things.[15]

Hence, while Watts promotes the role of the heart in the life of the Christian, he equally promotes the role of the mind. He criticizes those who say they love God but don't know Him very well. 'Love', he says, 'must be founded on knowledge'. Equally, he urges people that their knowledge of God should result in love: 'Knowledge and affection should go hand in hand'.

---

14   Ibid., 'The World to Come', Volume 1, p. 626.
15   Ibid., 'Love of God', Volume 2, p. 641.

Secondly, love for God flows specifically from knowledge of His mercy to us. Watts points out that the devil has very good knowledge of God, but he has no love for Him. The reason? It's because he knows there is no hope of mercy. We need to know God's goodness to us so that we respond in love to Him rather than in fear. We love Him because He first loved us.

This leads Watts to say that there are three key 'springs' for our love of God: 'a clear discovery of what God is in himself; a lively sense of what he has done for us; and a well grounded hope of what he will bestow upon us.' That is, God's character, God's actions and God's promises. Who God is, what He has done and what He will do for us. If we understand and see these things as we should, then we will know God and we will love Him. These things are made known to us most clearly in Jesus. So when Watts later considers how we might excite love for God in our hearts, the first thing he says is that we should reflect on these areas.

Thirdly, true love for God means we will choose Him. When we are presented with choices, we always choose what seems most desirable to us. So, true love for God means seeing Him as most desirable and most lovely. The battle for the Christian life is a battle of love. The world constantly calls us to love other things as most desirable, whether that's money or pleasure or comfort, or whatever draws our hearts. True love for God involves 'a choice of him above and beyond all things else, as our most desirable portion and our eternal good'.

Fourthly, love for God includes *feeling love* for Him. Remember, our minds and feelings are tied together, so we should feel something in our hearts, not just know something in our heads. This means there should be desire for God and delight in Him. Watts says:

> It is a vain thing for man to say, 'I love God with all my heart' when his strongest desires and most relishing joys centre in meaner objects; when his highest hopes and his most painful fears, his deepest anxieties and disquietudes of mind are always raised and sunk again by the things

of this world only, and the changing scenes of this mortal
state.[16]

In other words, if we end up feeling more strongly over the
up and downs of life, then we don't really love God with
all our heart.

Lastly, if we love God, it means that the rest of life will be
affected. Since the passions are the engine of life, supreme
love for God should become the motivational engine that
drives all that the Christian does:

> Where the love of God reigns in the affections...the eye
> will often look up to God in a way of faith and humble
> dependence; the ear will be attentive to his holy word; the
> hand will be lifted up to heaven in daily requests; the knee
> will be bended in humble worship; all the outward powers
> will be busy in doing the will of God and promoting his
> glory.[17]

Where love for God is absent, Watts sees the Christian
life as cool and dry and full of duty. It has no life or vigour
or power to it. By contrast, if the love of God is ruling in
the heart, then the engine of the Christian life is running
properly.

This understanding of the love of God has significant
implications. It means that love for God is the true fruit of
the gospel in our lives. We can evaluate how much someone
knows of God by his or her love for Him.

This means that good knowledge of God is vital – you
cannot love someone you don't know. But it also means
that right knowledge is not enough:

> Even where reason is bright and the judgment clear, yet
> it will be ineffectual for any valuable purposes, if religion
> reach no farther than the head, and proceed not to the
> heart: it will have but little influence if there are none of
> the passions engaged. ... Cold, unaffecting notions will
> have no powerful influence to reform our lives.[18]

---

16   Ibid., 'Love of God', Volume 2, pp. 656-7.

17   Ibid., 'Love of God', Volume 2, p. 643.

18   Ibid., 'Love of God', Volume 2, p. 663.

It is this love that distinguishes real Christianity from external hypocrisy. Watts says that hypocrites can perform many outward actions, but 'the various inward affections of nature, can never be kept in any steady and regular exercise of piety, by all the toil and skill of a hypocrite.' However, 'if the heart be thoroughly devoted to the love of God, this love will reign sovereign among the other passions.'

Also, remember that in Watts' understanding what we love and hate lies behind all our other passions. Our joy, fear, delight, hope, sadness, everything comes from what we love most. And so, he says, if we love God, it will guide our other passions, which are so often out of control:

> Now if we had but one sovereign bridle, that could reach and manage them all; one golden rein, that would hold in all their unruly motions, and would also excite and guide them at pleasure; what a valuable instrument this would be to mortals! Such an instrument is the love of God, such an invaluable regulator of all the passionate powers; and it will have this effect, where it is strong and supreme, as it ought to be.[19]

This means that if we truly know God and love God, then all our other emotions will get sorted out! Love of God 'in a sovereign manner rules and manages, awakens or suppresses all the other passions of the soul'.

Think of a marriage where one spouse truly loves the other. This will result in a whole variety of other emotions: hating the idea of offending them, rejoicing in what brings them pleasure, sadness over what hurts them, and so on. In a similar way, says Watts, love of God will result in admiration of God, desire for God, joy and pleasure in God, love of God's Word, love of God's people, love of God's Son, zeal for God, hatred for anything which offends God and fear of anything that would cut us off from God.

We might feel that Watts is setting a really high standard. In one sense he is, but he also gives lots of reassurances. He says again that people vary as to how much they feel and

---

19   Ibid., 'Love of God', Volume 2, p. 658.

that feelings vary over time. He says that physical things raise our emotions more easily than spiritual truths. He is more concerned that people focus on the *existence* of real love of God than *how much* they feel. So, he says, people should look to their desire to honour and obey God over time – 'these things are a better proof of true faith and real piety than a sudden flash of affection can be.'

Watts, then, was extremely concerned that there wasn't just assent to right belief. Rather, he wanted a beating heart, passionate for God. But neither was he after purely emotional religion. In fact, he thought that right love, stemming from right knowledge, would overflow into right living. Love for God was the crucial, and often missing, hinge between belief about God and living for God. And so we should ask: is that hinge missing today? Is that one reason why so many Christians feel 'underpowered' in their Christian walk? Are we not giving enough attention to growing in love? If so, what should we do?

Encouraging love of God

All of this means that Watts directs Christians as to how they can excite the love of God in their own hearts. If God is worthy of our love above all else, and if love for Him is key to living for Him, then we must give ourselves to growing in this love.

But how? This is where Watts gets really practical. He has lots of suggestions as to how to do this in practice. He says he will 'propose a few proper methods, whereby the affections of nature may be awakened and employed in the Christian life'. Here are some of them.

First, says Watts, as our passions come from what we know of something, we must give ourselves to knowing God and reflecting on Him. He says:

> Where the understanding has but a poor and scanty furniture of the things of God, the pious affections will have the fewer things to raise them.[20]

---

20   Ibid., 'Love of God', Volume 2, p. 704.

So, says Watts, don't think clear knowledge of God and warmth of heart to Him are opposed to each other. Clear knowledge is a spring to a warm heart. Watts encourages people to think deeply and clearly, so as to be able to love God more. In fact, he says, they should not be content with vague and unclear pictures of God, because we can't love something we don't see clearly.

Secondly, we should meditate on God: on His character, His works and His promises. This work of meditation is not learning new things but calling to mind what we know and bringing it home to our hearts. We should, above all, meditate on the cross of Christ. That is where we see God most clearly in His loving character and His promises of grace to us. There is link here with Watts' hymns – the most famous of which is 'When I survey the wondrous cross'. That hymn is a meditation on how we should think and feel when looking at the cross of Jesus.

Watts gives a flavour of the sorts of things we ought to be saying to ourselves in this type of meditation. Here's a brief taste:

> Enter into yourselves, think what you once were, corrupt, abominable, unclean, unholy. Remember the distinguishing grace of God, whereby you were awakened to a sense of your sin and danger, and were taught to fly for refuge to Jesus, your all sufficient hope. Think on your iniquities all pardoned; think of your garments and soul washed white in the blood of the lamb; think on the powerful influences of the Spirit, that has changed your vile nature, and made it holy, that has guarded you from a thousand temptations, and is training you up to everlasting blessedness. Which of the passions is there, that would lie cold and silent, under the lively sentiments of such a various and important scene of things?[21]

This is surely something we have to learn today. In a culture where everything is 'instant', and we love what is 'new', we have to learn to take the time to dwell on what is old and familiar so that it affects our hearts.

---

21   Ibid., 'Love of God', Volume 2, p. 707.

Thirdly, we should speak to God and express our affection for Him. Watts sees that actual practice of emotional expression to God itself has an effect on our hearts. In other words, we shouldn't wait until we feel love before we tell Him that we love Him. Rather, as we tell Him that we love Him, we will stir our love. Expression like this 'will keep all the passions in a habitual practice of religion, and maintain inward piety in the life and power of it'.

Watts particularly suggests using the parts of Scripture which are emotionally engaging. We should put that language on our own lips because expressing things like that will help us feel them. This is where Watts especially picks out the psalms. He calls them 'an altar of sacred fire'. He says:

> It is an example and a spring of most lively and exalted devotions... lift up your souls to God in the words of David, or imitate his language, where his words do not so perfectly express your case. Enter into his spirit, form and model your pious affections by that illustrious pattern.[22]

Fourthly, we must beware of our affections towards the world. We must be radical with what draws our hearts. Some things will be sinful and should not be indulged at all. Others will be perfectly lawful and even good, but we must beware they do not draw our love more than they should:

> Whenever you find a tempting creature taking too fast a hold of your passions, set a guard of sacred jealousy upon it, keep your heart at a holy distance from that creature, lest it twine about your inward powers, and draw them off from their allegiance and duty to God your creator.[23]

Fifthly, we should speak about God with other Christians to help each other stir up love for Him:

> Mutual conversation shall raise the divine flame higher, like united torches, which increase each other's blaze...

---

22   Ibid., 'Love of God', Volume 2, p. 708.
23   Ibid., 'Love of God', Volume 2, p. 705.

Man is a social creature, and his passions were made to be raised by converse.[24]

There's a challenge for us today: conversation with other Christians that makes us all feel more passionate about God at the end of it!

But ultimately, says Watts, we must look to God and pray for His work in us:

Seek earnestly the influences of the quickening Spirit. Without him you can do nothing. It is the Spirit of God who raises dead sinners at first into a divine life, and he puts all the languid springs of life into new motion... It is he who awakens our fear, who excites our hopes, who kindles our love and desire to things holy and heavenly; and it is he who exalts our spiritual joys.[25]

Christians, then, should give themselves to promoting the love of God in their own hearts.

Taking care

While Watts is keen to vindicate and encourage the affectionate Christian, he also gives a number of cautions. We said above he thinks 'enthusiasm' exists and is not a good thing. In light of this, he cautions people against making their passions a source of knowledge; or living by them and making decisions by them, as opposed to living by the truth.

He cautions people against good passions sliding into bad ones so that zeal for truth becomes indignation, hatred of sin becomes hatred of people, admiration becomes envy, and so on.

He cautions people about feeling something for God but it having no effect on their life:

What a reproach it is to the profession of the gospel to see a Christian just come from church and holy ordinances where his devout affections have been raised, and immediately to find him breaking out in vain, earthly

---

24 Ibid., 'Love of God', Volume 2, p. 709.
25 Ibid.

merriment and carried away with idle and sensual discourse.[26]

He especially cautions people against living for an experience of God so that they become dependent on particular kinds of experiences. He says of these Christians that they're always high as a kite, or low and depressed: they're never just steady. Here's how he puts it:

> Such Christians as these live very much by sudden fits and starts of devotion without that uniform and steady spring of faith and holiness ... they are always high on the wing, or else lying moveless on the ground; they are ever in the heights or the depths, travelling on bright mountains with the songs of heaven on their lips, or groaning and labouring through the dark valleys, and never walking onward as on an even plain, toward heaven.[27]

Watts speaks of those who have a particular experience such as 'a strong and divine impression from some particular scripture, or from some bright sentence in a sermon'. He doesn't put down these experiences or question their authenticity. His concern is simply that the person doesn't make such an experience a foundation for their faith. He says of one person: 'They have made this inward sensation the ground of their hope; they have fed still upon this cordial, and lived upon this support.' He goes on: 'When these extraordinary supplies fail them, they sink, and tremble, and die.'

All this means we must be very watchful over our own hearts:

> To guard against these dangers let Christians frequently enter into their own hearts and endeavour as far as possible to examine their own spirit and conscience, to distinguish between their inward workings of piety, and the mere exercises of animal nature, or the workings of corrupt affection, and set a constant guard on their hearts in this respect.[28]

---

26   Ibid., 'Love of God', Volume 2, p. 689.

27   Ibid., 'Love of God', Volume 2, p. 692.

28   Ibid., 'Love of God', Volume 2, p. 691.

Promoting the heart

I've said that Watts was writing at a time when religion had cooled. Enthusiasm was a danger to be wary of, but the majority position was cool, reasonable religion. In response, Watts promoted heart religion: experience of God and love for God.

We surely need to do the same. We need, as Watts did, an awareness of the dangers so that there is no promotion of emotionalism, in fact, so that there is a countering of that. But we must insist that good understanding, while necessary, is not enough. Seeing God clearly must lead to loving God deeply. Loving Him deeply leads to living for Him well.

This kind of thinking needs to be promoted in our churches today.

7
HUMBLY WORKING FOR REVIVAL

We've seen that religion was in a pretty poor state in the first decades of the eighteenth century. The role of reason had been exalted and religion had cooled. People might still state the truths of the gospel, but they were mostly concerned with being seen to be rational, not passionate, about them. We have also seen how Isaac Watts welcomed advances in reason and yet also longed for a revival of heartfelt religion. He saw this revival as involving three key areas: preaching, prayer and praise. Watts comments on an event in Acts 2 which he sees as a model of church life. In that chapter, the apostles preach to the believers; they all pray together, and a psalm is quoted (which Watts takes as evidence of singing). Watts says of this moment:

> May these ears of mine be entertained with such devotion in public, such prayer, such preaching, and such praise! May these eyes behold such returning glory in the churches![1]

This is what Watts worked for – a return of God's glory in the church. This is what he longed for – revival by the reforming of the church. In the next chapter, we will examine how he contributed to a reformation of the praise of the church. Before we do that, we'll look at his work on preaching and prayer.

---

1   Ibid., 'Improvement of Psalmody', Volume 4, p. 281.

An humble attempt

In 1730, a minister, Strickland Gough, published a book called *An Enquiry into the Causes of the Decay of the Dissenting Interest*. In other words – why are the dissenting churches shrinking? He argued that dissent had lost its primary conviction over liberty of conscience. Instead, dissenting churches had become arrogant and not allowed each other true freedom to worship. He also said that dissenters managed their affairs very badly and were disorderly, which meant people were drawn to the calm efficiency of the state church.

There were a number of replies to Gough, including one by Watts' friend Philip Doddridge. But in 1731 Watts wrote himself. It was called *An Humble Attempt towards the Revival of Practical Religion among Christians*. Some of the material had originally been written as a sermon for the ordination of a minister. However, Watts was prevented from preaching by illness. Instead, he expanded and published his thoughts.

Watts accepted some of Gough's points but argued that the key issue in the decay of religion is not to do with external organization but with the vitality of heart religion. In his first lines, he simply stated: 'the great and general reason is the decay of vital religion in the heart and lives of men.'

The book addresses ministers and then congregations. It is wide-ranging in its topics and calls people to embrace all the advantages of dissent – which Watts thinks are significant. But this is to be done with the aim of growth in the knowledge and love of God, and of living out a real relationship with Him. All the benefits and freedom of dissent must be used to grow in 'vital religion'. This is seen especially in Watts' view of preaching and prayer.

The state of preaching

In the previous century, preaching could be divided into two well-known types. There was what was called 'baroque' preaching. This was preaching as performance. The aim was to show off your learning, and the content was adjusted to fit a clever rhetorical scheme rather than to help people know God.

By contrast, the Puritan style of preaching focused on straightforward presentation of Biblical truth applied to people's lives. The best of these were fantastic. The worst had good content but were pretty dull. The Puritan sermon was known for 'branching': that is, dividing the content into headings and subheadings. This could give the sermon great clarity, but too many 'branches' meant it became overly complicated.

By the eighteenth century, though, both these styles were out of favour. The sermons of the day naturally reflected the religious mood of the day. As we have seen, that mood called for reasoned explanation and for a religion focused on morality. Not surprisingly, in came preaching marked by reason and clarity, usually aimed at promoting moral living rather than the acts of God in salvation. In this increasingly scientific and rational culture, passionate rhetoric was regarded suspiciously. It was seen as the use of words to mislead people. So, along with straightforward explanation there must not be any attempt to stir people's emotions! The result was sermons which sounded more like lectures being read rather than the Word of God being preached.

Daniel Defoe compared the dissenting preaching of his day with the Puritans of the previous century, saying that the Puritans:

> ... preached their sermons, rather than read them in the pulpit; they spoke from the heart to the heart, nothing like our cold declaiming way, entertained now as a mode, and read with a flourish.[2]

Watts and the art of preaching

Watts was from a Puritan background, but he didn't want simply a return to Puritan preaching. In fact, he was

---

2   Daniel Defoe, *The Present State of the Parties in Great Britain: Particularly an Enquiry into the State of the Dissenters in England* (London: J. Baker, 1712), p. 289.

critical of the classic Puritan sermon: he refers to preachers drawing up their list of points to 'eighteenthly or seven and twentiethly'! He compares their numerous sub-points to Ezekiel's vision of dry bones and says, 'There were very many in the valley, and lo, they were very dry.' However, he also points out that these sermons contained substantial doctrine aimed at people's good and growth; this, he says, must be recovered.

But Watts was more critical of the dry and moral preaching around him. This was considered good oratory: it didn't use any headings because that would have broken up the flow. It was more concerned with people being carried along by the words than with grasping truth. Watts says it 'glides over the ear like a rivulet of oil over polished marble, and like that too, leaves no trace behind it'. The listener may be 'pleased perhaps with the music of your voice as with the sound of a sweet instrument, and they mistook that for devotion; but their heads are dark still, and their hearts earthly.'

In other words, while this kind of preaching is pleasant to listen to, it has no effect on people's hearts. Watts' main concern is that it makes no lasting impression on the listeners, so nothing is achieved:

> Can a long purling sound awaken a sleepy conscience, and give a perishing sinner just notions of his dreadful hazard? Can it furnish his understanding and memory with all the awesome and tremendous topics of our religion, when it scarcely leaves any distinct impression of one of them in his soul? Can you make the arrow wound where it will not stick? Where the discourse vanishes from the remembrance can you suppose the soul to be profited or enriched? When you brush over the closed eyelids with a feather, did you ever find it give light to the blind? Have any of your soft discourses, your continued threads of silken eloquence ever raised the dead?[3]

Watts' great concern in preaching was that people encounter God's truth in a way that engages their minds

---

3   Watts, *Works*, 'Improvement', Volume 5, p. 349.

and penetrates their hearts. So, in speaking to preachers in his *Humble Attempt*, Watts says:

> Do not say within yourself, How much or how elegantly can I talk upon such a text, but, What can I say most usefully to those who hear me, for the instruction of their minds, for the conviction of their consciences, and for the persuasion of their hearts... not what fine things can I say, either in way of criticism or philosophy, or in way of oratory or discourse, but what powerful words can I speak to impress the consciences of them that hear with a serious and lasting sense of moral, divine and eternal things?[4]

He says elsewhere to those listening to sermons:

> We are too often ready to judge that to be the best sermon, which has many strange thoughts in it, many fine hints, and some grand and polite sentiments. But a Christian in his best temper of mind will say, 'That is a good sermon which brings my heart nearer to God, which makes the grace of Christ sweet to my soul, and the commands of Christ easy and delightful'.[5]

Watts then argues for preaching which contains the solid doctrine of the Puritans but delivers this in a way which is accessible and vibrant to the listener. This means making fewer points, but making them well! Referring back to the branching sermon as being like Ezekiel's valley of dry bones, Watts goes on:

> It is the variety of enlargement upon a few proper heads that clothes the dry bones with flesh, and animates them with blood and spirits; it is this that colours the discourse, makes it warm and strong, and renders the divine propositions bright and persuasive. It is this that brings down the doctrine or the duty to the understanding and the conscience of the whole congregation, and commands the natural affections into the interest of the gospel. In short it is this, which under the influence of the Holy Spirit, gives life and force, beauty and success to a sermon,

---

4   Ibid., 'Humble Attempt', Volume 3, p. 8.
5   Ibid., 'Sermons', Volume 1, p. xxvi.

and provides food for souls. A single rose bush or a dwarf pear, with all their leaves, flowers and fruit about them have more beauty and spirit in themselves, and yield more food and pleasure to mankind than the innumerable branches, boughs and twigs of a long hedge of thorns.[6]

The need for clarity

We can focus on two key elements for Watts in preaching. The first is clarity. This is where he agreed with much of the thought of his day: he agreed that some previous preaching was too complicated, used too much theological language, and sometimes covered over difficulties with doctrinal terms. Instead, said Watts, let's say what we mean and mean what we say.

Thus, Watts spoke of the need for clear and plain language. This, he said, was difficult to achieve in practice. In fact, he wrote a short poem to that effect:

Smooth be your style, and plain and natural,
To strike the sons of Wapping or Whitehall.
While others think this easy to attain,
Let them but try, and with their utmost pain
They'll sweat and strive to imitate in vain.[7]

This meant that preachers needed to develop a clear style which conveyed to the listener exactly what was in the preacher's own mind:

Seek to obtain a perspicuous style and a clear and distinct manner of speaking, that you may effectually impress the understanding, while you pronounce the words; that you may so exactly imprint on the mind of the hearers, the same ideas which you have conceived, that they may never mistake your meaning.[8]

This need for clarity also influenced the structure of sermons. Headings were not regarded as part of 'polite'

---

6   Ibid., 'Improvement', Volume 5, p. 348.

7   Ibid., 'Improvement', Volume 5, pp. 347-8. The last lines of this are a translation from Horace.

8   Ibid., 'Humble Attempt', Volume 3, p. 20.

preaching, but Watts didn't care. He said that preachers should order their material clearly and use headings to aid the memory of their congregations. Watts' own sermons had no one structure, but he commonly followed the model of establishing a doctrine and then applying it. In the application section, he recommends speaking directly to different categories of listener.

Here's an example from a sermon on the atonement of Christ:

1. To explain more at large the manner in which I conceive Christ to become an atonement or propitiation for our sins.

2. To give some reasons to prove, that he is ordained of God, and set forth or offered to the world under this character,

3. I shall show what glorious use is made of this doctrine throughout the whole Christian life.

For Watts, everything in the preacher's use of language and structure was to help the understanding of the hearer. He emphasizes:

You must break the bread of life into pieces to feed children with it, and part your discourses into distinct propositions to give the ignorant a plain scheme of any one doctrine, and enable them to comprehend or retain it.[9]

Watts also asserted that people must not simply feel something when hearing a sermon; they must be convinced in their own mind. And so the logic of a sermon must be compelling:

Since you have to do with reasonable creatures in your sacred work, let your manner of speaking be rational, and your arguments and inferences just and strong; that you may effectually convince your hearers of the truth of what you deliver, in your ministrations of the gospel.[10]

---

9   Ibid., 'Improvement', Volume 5, p. 350.
10   Ibid., 'Humble Attempt', Volume 3, p. 20.

This concern for clarity and the use of logic did not mean that Watts thought the preacher could persuade people himself, though. Rather, every preacher was completely dependent on the work of the Holy Spirit. This was true even for the preacher in his own study who was composing sermons:

> ... seek the direction and assistance of the Spirit of God, for inclining your thoughts to proper subjects, for guiding you to proper Scriptures and framing your whole sermon both as to the matter and manner that it may attain the divine and sacred ends proposed.[11]

It was also true for the effect of a sermon on the listeners: 'without the influences of the Spirit of God, it will have little effect to draw sinners unto Christ.' Because of this, Watts urged preachers to call on God:

> If we should have reason to fear that the Spirit of God is much departed from others, let us cry with great earnestness, that the Spirit may never leave our assemblies, and abandon us to labour in vain without his influences.[12]

The need for passion

While Watts was keen to urge clarity in preaching, he was just as equally concerned to urge passion. This should not surprise us given what we saw him say about heartfelt religion. To revive heartfelt religion among the congregation, said Watts, we must have heartfelt preaching.

Watts had a number of recommendations to achieve this. First, he emphasized the need for the preacher to have vital, heartfelt religion himself. This meant regular examination of the affections of the preacher. For example:

> Call your own soul often to account; examine the temper, the frame and the motions of your own heart with all holy severity. ... Be tenderly aware of every wandering affection toward vanity, every deviation from God and your duty,

11 Ibid., 'Humble Attempt', Volume 3, p. 7.
12 Ibid., 'Rational Foundation', Volume 6, p. 109.

every rising sin, every degree of growing distance from God.[13]

The result, says Watts, will be shown in all the minister's duties, but especially in his preaching: 'a word coming from the heart will sooner reach the heart.' Secondly, as well as persuasive logic, there must also be passionate appeal:

> A mere conviction of the reason and judgment, by the strongest arguments, is hardly sufficient, in matters of piety and virtue, to command the will into obedience; because the appetites of the flesh, and the interests of the world are engaged on the opposite side. ... The God of nature therefore has furnished mankind with those powers, which we call passions, or affections of the heart, in order to excite the will with superior vigour and activity to avoid the evil and pursue the good. Upon this account the preacher must learn to address the passions in a proper manner...[14]

This has huge implications for how pastors preach. They must:

> ... contrive all lively, forcible and penetrating forms of speech, to make your words powerful and impressive on the hearts of your hearers, when light is first let into the mind. Practise all the awful and solemn ways of address to the conscience, all the soft and tender influences on the heart.[15]

We noted earlier that in Watts' day people were wary of passionate rhetoric in sermons; they thought that rhetorical flourishes were used to cover bad argument and could mislead people. Watts, by contrast, thought that passionate rhetoric was desperately needed:

> The movements of sacred passion may be the ridicule of an age which pretends to nothing but calm reasoning. Life

---

13 Ibid., 'Humble Attempt', Volume 3, p. 3.

14 Ibid., 'Humble Attempt', Volume 3, p. 22.

15 Ibid.

and zeal in the ministry of the word may be despised by men of lukewarm and dying religion... But this very life and zeal, this sacred fervency, shall still remain one bright character of the Christian preacher, till the names of Paul and Apollos perish from the church; and that is, till this Bible and these heavens are no more.[16]

Watts reminds preachers that they must still be clear and logical, but only passionate preaching will touch people in their sin:

The understanding indeed ought to be first convinced by the plainest and strongest force of reasoning; but when this is done, all the powerful motives should be used which have any just influence on human nature, all the springs of passion should be touched, to awaken the stupid and the thoughtless into consideration, to penetrate and melt the hardest heart, to persuade the unwilling, to excite the lazy, to reclaim the obstinate, and to reform the vicious part of mankind, as well as to encourage those who are humble and pious, and to support their practice and their hope.[17]

Watts himself, then, uses impassioned language, especially within his 'application' section of a sermon. For example, in the sermon mentioned above on the atonement of Christ, within the application section, Watts says this doctrine should be a powerful motive for repentance and forgiveness. He goes on:

And is there such an atonement made? And are there such pardons provided for such guilty wretches as I have been? Is God reconciling himself to men, and reconciling men to himself, by the blood of Jesus? Then let my soul mourn for all her follies, her past iniquities. Let me be covered with shame, and lie in the dust at the foot of God. O let him speak forgiveness and peace to me...[18]

This also influenced how Watts recommended that people deliver their sermons. The standard method of delivery of

---

16   Ibid., 'Sermons', Volume 1, pp. xxi-xxii.
17   Ibid., 'Improvement', Volume 5, p. 312.
18   Ibid., 'Sermons', Volume 1, pp. 396-7.

the rational sermon was to read a prepared manuscript. Watts, by contrast, recommended preparing headings but then speaking extempore. This was especially so that the preacher might express his passion more easily, which Watts thought a prepared manuscript would restrict.

We should not impose on ourselves just such a number of pre-composed words and lines to be delivered in the hour, without daring to speak a warm sentiment that comes fresh upon the mind. Why may you not hope for some lively turns of thought, some new pious sentiments which may strike light, and heat, and life into the understandings and the hearts of those that hear you?[19]

The preacher should also avoid any hint of coldness or indifference but rather take joy in his task so as to affect the congregation: 'Stir yourself up to the work with sacred vigour that the assembly may feel what you speak.' The preacher should try to get his own heart into a 'temper of divine love' where he longs for God's honour and feels for lost sinners. There should be a great sense of the gravity of the situation, and Watts echoes the Puritan Richard Baxter in saying, 'Speak as a dying preacher to dying hearers.'[20]

For Watts, the passion of the preacher is key to his congregation's response:

When the words freeze upon his lips, the hearts of his hearers are freezing also: But where we find devout affection mingled with solid argument in the discourse, there the lips of the preacher seem to speak light and life at once, and he helps to communicate the holy passion all around him, by feeling it first himself.[21]

This all leads Watts to reject the cool, rational preaching of his day:

Can we be content any longer to be the cold and lifeless rehearsers of the great and glorious things of our religion?

---

19   Ibid., 'Humble Attempt', Volume 3, p. 27.
20   Baxter's famous line was that he preached, 'As a dying man to dying men'.
21   Watts, *Works*, 'Love of God', Volume 2, p. 679.

Can we go on to speak to perishing sinners, who lie
drowsy and slumbering on the brink of hell, in so soft,
so calm and gentle a manner, as though we were afraid
to awaken them? ... Who taught us any of this lazy and
drowsy practice? Did God or his prophets, did *Christ* or
his apostles, instruct in this modish art of still life, this
lethargy of preaching...? Did the great God ever appoint
statues for his ambassadors, to invite sinners to his mercy?
Words of grace written upon brass or marble would do
the work almost as well. Where the preachers become
stone, no wonder if the hearers are motionless. But let
the ministers of the living word who address men upon
matters of infinite concern show, if possible, that they are
infinitely concerned about them.[22]

This observation was made of Watts' own manner in the
pulpit:

Though his stature was low and his bodily presence but
weak, yet his preaching was weighty and powerful. There
was a certain dignity and respect in his very aspect which
commanded attention and awe, and when he spoke, such
strains of truly Christian eloquence flowed from his lips, and
these so apparently animated with zeal for God, and the most
tender concern for souls, and their everlasting salvation, as
one would think could not be easily slighted or resisted.[23]

Watts longed for revival of the church to come through
the reformation of preaching. He did not argue simply
for a return to the Puritan style of preaching of a century
earlier. His appreciation of the new logic of his day meant
he wanted a more streamlined style. But he remained
Puritan at heart in wanting preaching that declared the
great truths of Scripture and did so in a way that touched
people's hearts.

The argument over prayer
People argued over prayer a great deal in the eighteenth
century; arguments which were a carry-over from the

22 Ibid., 'Love of God', Volume 2, p. 678.
23 David Jennings, *A Funeral Sermon for the Late Reverend Isaac Watts D.D.*
    (London: Oswald and Dilly, 1749), p. 32.

previous century. Back in the seventeenth century, there were huge debates over the Prayer Book which was used in the Church of England. Puritans had fought to change the content of that book to make it more Biblical. However, others had argued that there should not be such a book at all, especially that prayers should not be 'set' by being written down and then read out. The battle lines then were that some argued for 'set' prayers, while others wanted 'free' prayer.

One side said that set prayers were too impersonal, they made the words of the particular prayer chosen too important, they led to hypocrisy and they robbed the congregation of the gift of addressing God in their own words. The reply from those in favour of set prayers was that spontaneous prayer gave no thought to what was being said, it gave the people listening no opportunity to evaluate what was being said and that it often resulted in prayers being a show by the person praying.

Some arguments were thoughtful and respectful. Some weren't. The set prayer group were accused of quenching the Spirit. The free prayer group were said to pray 'extempore gibberish'.

We should be aware in all this that prayer had a much more prominent part in a regular Sunday service than it usually does today. It was usually conducted by the pastor and was of considerable length. Some pastors were known as much for their public praying as they were for their preaching.

At Watts' own church, we are told that in the 'main prayer':

> ... the minister prays more at large, for all the variety of blessings, spiritual and temporal, for the whole congregation, with confession of sins, and thanksgiving for mercies; petitions also are offered up for the whole world, for the churches of Christ, for the nation in which we dwell, for all our rulers and governors, together with any particular cases which are represented.[24]

---

24   'Transactions of the Congregational Historical Society,' VI (1913-15): p. 334.

Watts and practice of prayer

Watts speaks about the conduct of prayer in his *Humble Attempt*. However, he had earlier produced *A Guide to Prayer* in 1715. In the preface of *A Guide*, he is straightforward about the fact that public prayer in the churches needs to be revised. He has written his book, he says, not to explain the doctrine of prayer, but to give a guide to how it should be practised. The *Guide*, then, is designed to be a manual for the help of average Christians in their prayer life, but also for the reform of public prayer in churches.

Watts defines prayer as including all addresses between man and God, rather than being limited to petition. He says:

> It is that language, wherein a creature holds correspondence with his creator: and wherein the soul of a saint often gets near to God, is entertained with great delight, and, as it were, dwells with his heavenly father for a short season before he comes to heaven.[25]

Watts discusses the different parts to prayer. He identifies nine such parts: invocation, adoration, confession, petition, pleading, profession or dedication, thanksgiving, blessing, and 'the Amen' or conclusion. For each of these, he describes what we are doing in it and gives expressions, often from the Bible, which can be used. Just reading through these sections and the way Watts describes them would make most of us realize the shallow nature of our prayers!

The next chapters describe the 'gift', 'grace' and 'spirit' of prayer. The gift of prayer is our ability to phrase our prayers to rightly suit what it is we want to say in appropriate language. This is the outward nature of prayer. By contrast, the grace of prayer is the heart attitude which lies behind such prayer and which requires God's work in our hearts.

The spirit of prayer, then, refers to the work of the Holy Spirit helping Christians to gain the gift and grace

---

25   Watts, *Works*, 'Prayer', Volume 3, p. 109.

of prayer. In Watts' day, some people said the Spirit lay behind all of prayer and so they could simply rely on Him. Others played down the role of the Spirit, saying that our prayers were our own work. Watts is critical of both these positions, saying that we must and can work at prayer, but that the Spirit must be at work in us.

Freedom or set forms?

Watts is well aware of all the arguments there have been over set forms of prayer. He makes this comment on the situation:

> But if the leaders of one party had spent as much time in learning to pray, as they have done in reading liturgies, and vindicating their imposition; and if the warm writers of the other side, together with their just cautions against quenching the spirit, had more cultivated this divine skill themselves, and taught Christians regularly how to pray; I believe the practice of free-prayer had been more universally approved, and the fire of this controversy had never raged to the destruction of so much charity.[26]

In other words, both sides had something right. The free prayer group were often slapdash in their prayers and should have paid more attention to the words they use and how they prayed. But the set prayer group should have grown in the skill of prayer for themselves rather than relying on only set prayers.

Watts describes his position and aim:

> My design in this treatise has been to write a prayer-book without forms. And I have sought to maintain the middle way between the distant mistakes of contending Christians.[27]

So, Watts lands firmly on the side of free prayer. However, he distances himself from some of the free prayer group. He distinguishes between free prayer which is 'spontaneous' as opposed to that which is 'prepared'. By 'prepared', Watts

---

26   Ibid., 'Prayer', Volume 3, p. 106.
27   Ibid.

means it has been carefully thought over and considered but has not been committed to a set form of words such that it will be read out. He is very concerned that public prayer in church uses prepared prayer, rather than either spontaneous or set. This is what he means above by seeking a 'middle way'.

It's not that Watts thinks set prayers are completely wrong. In fact, he is happy that people use them on occasion if they find them helpful. And he wrote prayers for children, which involved writing set forms to be read. Here's how he stated the issue:

> It is not our own composing of a prayer, nor the reading of a prayer composed, nor the saying it over without a book, or repeating it after another, that is either necessary or sinful in itself: But it is the understanding and the inward desire and affection accompanying the words, that render the work of prayer pleasing to God: And it is the want of that understanding, desire and affection, that will spoil all pretences to devotion, whether the words be read or said without book.[28]

Notice the key elements: clear understanding and appropriate affection. Watts is less concerned with the words we use than whether we understand what we say and that we feel what we say. He hates the idea of prayer that is either mindless or heartless (or both).

However, for such good understanding and appropriate feeling, Watts believes that set prayers are not usually the best option. They can be good for children who are learning how to pray, and they can help adults when we feel stuck in prayer. But using our own words to express our own situation and experience will help with the key elements of mind and heart in prayer. So, he says of praying in the general terms of set prayers:

> ... generals are cold and do not affect us, nor affect persons that join with us, and whose case he that speaks in prayer should represent before God. It is much sweeter

---

28   Ibid., 'Prayers for Children', Volume 3, p. 502.

to our own souls, and to our fellow-worshippers, to have our fears, and doubts, and complaints, and temptations, and sorrows represented in most exact and particular expressions, in such language as the soul itself feels when the words are spoken.[29]

Praying with mind and heart

Mind and heart then are crucial for Watts. This is why when he wrote prayers for children he carefully judged what was appropriate for each age group. He hated the idea that children would be taught to pray words that they did not understand. But the same is true for adults. Watts warns against people using scriptural phrases which aren't clear, or using theological language which people don't understand. He knows that in the nonconformist world those who are more 'enthusiastic' can easily sound ecstatic in their prayers but those listening have no idea what they are saying. This is, he says, 'sound without sense'. And that does no one any good.

We must use words carefully, says Watts, because they 'are useful, not only to dress our thoughts, but sometimes to form and shape, and perfect the ideas and affections of our minds'. That is, our words help us know what we mean and what we feel.

Watts knows, of course, that sometimes prayer can be expressed as a 'groan' or a 'cry', but in public prayer he wants people to use words and frame their prayers well. This means he gives practical advice such as avoiding overly long sentences, not using complicated words and structuring prayers in a logical order.

That order includes the connection between the mind and the heart. We should consider the truth we are praying about and then express how we feel about it:

> Let those things, in every part of prayer, which are the proper objects of our judgment, be first mentioned, and then those that influence and move our affections... there is occasion frequently in prayer, under the several parts

---

29   Ibid., 'Prayer', Volume 3, p. 126.

of it, for the recollecting of divine truths, and these lay a proper foundation for warm and heartfelt expressions to follow.[30]

The need for feeling in what we pray lies behind Watts' concern not to be tied to set forms:

... while we bind ourselves to those words only, we damp our inward devotion, and prevent the holy fire from kindling within us; we discourage our active powers and passions from running out on divine subjects, and check the breathing of our souls heaven-ward.[31]

He links this with the work of Spirit. The Spirit is the source of all our godly desires and feelings, and so we should express them in our words:

The thoughts and affections of the hearts that are truly pious and sincere are wrought in us by the Spirit of God, and if we deny them utterance because they are not found in prayer-books, we run the danger of resisting the Holy Ghost.[32]

In his *Humble Attempt*, this results in Watts exhorting dissenters to make the most of this advantage of freedom in prayer:

Are you more lively in the freer addresses of your souls to heaven without a confinement to set words and phrases? Are your spirits more humble, and your devotional thoughts in warmer exercise, while you are adoring the great and blessed God in a larger variety of language? Are your hearts more deeply affected...?[33]

For Watts, this means prayer can be a wonderfully moving and profound time:

When our souls are filled with a lively impression of some of the attributes, or works of God, when our hearts are

---

30   Ibid., 'Prayer', Volume 3, p. 138.
31   Ibid., 'Prayer', Volume 3, pp. 124-5.
32   Ibid., 'Prayer', Volume 3, p. 125.
33   Ibid., 'Humble Attempt', Volume 3, p. 58.

overpowered with a sense of our own guilt and unworthiness, or big with some important request; O what a blessed pleasure it is to hit upon a happy expression, that speaks our very soul, and fulfils all our meaning! And what a pleasure doth it convey to all that join with us, who have their spiritual senses exercised? And it helps to excite in them the same devotion that dictated to us the words we speak.[34]

This means that, just as we saw with preaching, the person leading in prayer should seek to express themselves in appropriate heartfelt ways, rather than remaining 'cool':

Seek after those ways of expression that are heartfelt, that denote the fervency of affection, and carry life and spirit with them; such as may awaken and exercise our love, our hope, our holy joy, our sorrow, our fear, and our faith, as well as express the activity of those graces. This is the way to raise, assist and maintain devotion.[35]

Watts also guides people in what we should feel during different parts of a prayer. For example, when confessing sin, we should try to express our sense of guilt and humility; when thanking God for salvation, we should speak with joy, and so on. Here's his section on when we are adoring God for His attributes:

The work of adoration or praise runs through the several attributes of the divine nature, and requires of us the exercise of our various affections suited to those several attributes. As when we mention God's self-sufficiency and independency, it becomes us to be humble and acknowledge our dependence: when we speak of his power, and of his wisdom, we should abase ourselves before him... When we mention his love and compassion, our souls should return much love to him, and have our affections going forth strongly towards him.[36]

As with preaching again, the person leading others in prayer should also be concerned with the state of his heart

---

34   Ibid., 'Prayer', Volume 3, p. 143.
35   Ibid., 'Prayer', Volume 3, p.146.
36   Ibid., 'Prayer', Volume 3, pp. 162-3.

before God; this too will help with appropriate expression and emotion:

> The passions of the mind, when they are moved, do mightily help the tongue. They fill the mouth with arguments; they give a natural eloquence to those who know not any rules of art; and they almost constrain the dumb to speak.[37]

Watts is very aware, though, that not everyone will feel what they might think they should or want to. This leads him to give a caution and comfort. The caution is not to read too much into the presence of certain feelings; the comfort is that we can still be sincere even when not feeling all that we think we should. He says: 'all the graces of prayer are seldom at work in the soul at once, in an eminent and conscious degree' because of our 'feeble and imperfect state'.

Work of people and the Spirit

Watts, then, wants people to work hard at praying well. He says prayer is a 'holy skill' and he is concerned that in his own grouping, the dissenters, there is not much skill in evidence. So, he says prayer is something we can get better at:

> As the art of medicine or healing is founded on the knowledge of natural principles, and made up of several rules drawn from the nature of things, from reason and observation ... so the holy skill of prayer is built on a just knowledge of God and ourselves, and may be taught in as rational a method by proper directions and rules.[38]

However, he also believes that we need the Spirit to work in us. The Spirit gives the inward reality and desire so important in prayer:

> When sin is recollected, he awakens anger, shame and sorrow. When God is revealed to the mind in his glory and

---

37   Ibid., 'Prayer', Volume 3, p. 140.
38   Ibid., 'Prayer', Volume 3, p. 123.

justice, he overspreads the soul with holy awe, and humble fear. When the Lord Jesus Christ, and his redemption, are upon the thoughts, the Holy Spirit warms and raises our desire and love. We are in ourselves cold and dead to spiritual things. He makes us lively in prayer, and holds us to the work; he begets a holy reverence of God while we adore him; he works in us delight in God and longing desires after him.[39]

So, Watts argued for a reformation in prayer. He wanted prayer that was clear and that was warm. He wanted people who had considered what they were going to pray, and how; people whose own hearts were warmed by those truths, who would then lead people in what they should think and what they should feel.

Preaching, prayer and revival

Watts saw preaching and prayer as key for the health of the church and so for the reviving of the church in his day.

Watts says of his own sermons:

I have not entertained you with lectures of philosophy, instead with the gospel of Christ; nor have I affected that easy indolence of style which is the dry delight of some modish writers, the cold and insipid pleasure of men who pretend to politeness. You know it has always been the business of my ministry to convince and persuade your souls in practical godliness, by the clearest and strongest reasons derived from the gospel, and by all the most moving methods of speech, of which I was capable; but still in a humble subserviency to the promised influences of the Holy Spirit.[40]

That is a great thing for a preacher to be able to say, and an excellent model for preachers to work towards today.

Watts speaks equally passionately about the need for improvement in prayer. He says that if we would learn this holy skill:

---

39   Ibid., 'Prayer', Volume 3, p. 176.
40   Ibid., 'Sermons', Volume 1, p. xxi.

Then shall they learn the perfection of beauty in this part of worship, when the gift and grace of prayer are happily joined in the secret pleasure and success of it, and appear before men in its full loveliness, and attractive power. Then shall religion look like itself, divine and heavenly, and shine in all the lustre it is capable of here on earth.[41]

Ultimately, of course, for such revival to come, God would have to work. Watts pleaded with ministers:

> Let us strive mightily in prayer and in preaching to revive the work of God, and beg earnestly that God, by a fresh and abundant work of his own Spirit, would revive his own work among us. Revive thy own Work, O Lord, in the midst of these Years of Sin and Degeneracy, nor let us labour in vain.[42]

---

41   Ibid., 'Prayer', Volume 3, p. 197.
42   Ibid., 'Humble Attempt', Volume 3, p. 125.

8
SINGING GOD'S PRAISE

Isaac Watts' true genius lay in hymn writing – it is no accident that this is what he is known for today. What is very important to do, though, is not simply to appreciate his great hymns, but also to appreciate why he wrote them, and why he wrote them the way he did. If we can do that rather than just continuing to sing some of his hymns (which we should), we will learn about his understanding of praise. That will be a lesson we can apply to whatever we sing.

Singing psalms
As Watts grew up, singing in church was very different than it is today! There were two big questions being debated. The first was: *should we sing* at all? Some said 'No' to this because they felt singing was asking people to take words on their lips which they might not believe. There were lots of people in church each week who weren't converted. So, some churches decided they shouldn't sing at all – otherwise non-Christians would be led to say things they didn't believe. The majority, however, did sing.

The second big question, for those who had decided singing was still OK to do, was: *what should we sing?* The answer was obvious: the Psalms from the Old Testament! The Psalms were seen to be God's own inspired hymn book, and if God has given His church a hymn book, why would one sing anything else? In fact, singing anything else would be wrong! The Puritans in England had been very influenced by John Calvin in this area. Calvin had argued for psalm-singing in Geneva, and various Englishmen had brought back the idea and the arguments with them. In the Church of England, other pieces of music were sung, often with trained choirs. But in nonconformist circles, psalm-singing ruled the day.

So, the Psalms were translated and made 'metrical', that is given a regular metre so that they would fit well-known tunes. But these metrical psalms had two main problems. The first was that they didn't let Christians sing of Jesus, the cross, the resurrection, the work of the Spirit and more. This lack of explicitly Christian lyrics was felt especially when it came to the Lord's Supper where Psalm 22 (as a prediction of the cross) was rather overused!

The result of this was that some had written new hymns for churches to sing as an addition to the psalms. This is important to note, as it means that Watts wasn't, as some say, the first to introduce new hymns. His title as 'the father of hymnody' comes not because he was the first but because he went further and wrote better than those before him. Before him was a trickle of new hymns; but he broke the dam.

The second problem with the metrical psalms was simply that they weren't very good! Watts commented on the singing of the church at the turn of the century, saying that the church 'ventures to sing a dull hymn or two at church, in tunes of equal dullness'.

Watts' brother wrote to him in 1700 encouraging him to publish some of the hymns that he had written. He refers to some of the recent authors of metrical psalms and says, 'Mason now reduces this kind of writing to a sort of yawning indifference, and honest Barton chimes us asleep.'[1]

It is generally accepted that of all the parts of corporate worship at the start of the eighteenth century, it was

---

1   Thomas Milner, *The Life, Times and Correspondence of the Rev. Isaac Watts, D.D.* (London: Simpkin and Marshall, 1834), p. 177.

singing that was performed worst. One writer says: 'The awkward inversions and plodding progression of their sad doggerel were calculated to dampen the ardour of the most enthusiastic singers.'[2]

The stage was set for Watts to bring a revolution.

Watts' programme of reform

Watts knew what he wanted to achieve in this area, and it was nothing less than the 'reformation of psalmody amongst the churches'. His reform began with the publishing of *Hymns and Spiritual Songs* in 1707; it was revised two years later and went through an enormous number of editions. This work was newly composed hymns rather than psalms and was divided into three sections: there were 'hymns collected from the scriptures' (for those who felt that hymns should only be based on the words of the Bible); 'hymns composed on divine subjects' (which were freer compositions); and 'hymns prepared for the Lord's Supper' (which met the felt need for suitable hymns focusing on remembering the cross).

Very soon these new hymns were being sung by dissenting congregations as additions to the metrical psalms already available. Watts had continued to encourage the singing of psalms but he intended to reform this area as well – which was far more controversial. So, in 1719 he published *The Psalms of David Imitated in the Language of the New Testament*. The title of this is significant. Watts hadn't simply written his own version of metrical psalms. Rather, he had paraphrased the psalms in the language of the New Testament – he had taken the liberty of 'updating' the psalms! We'll look at why and how he did this below.

In the prefaces to both his *Hymns* and *Psalms,* Watts explained his approach in writing. He also felt the need to defend himself, and with good reason! Especially with his *Psalms*, he was accused of thinking he could write better hymns than the Holy Spirit! This meant he also wrote an

2   Horton Davies, *Worship and Theology in England: Volume 3, From Watts and Wesley to Maurice, 1690-1850* (Princeton: Princeton University Press, 1961), p. 65.

Essay towards the Improvement of Christian Psalmody, which contains fuller arguments as to why we should not simply sing metrical psalms.

As we've mentioned, the idea of hymns supplementing the use of metrical psalms was more widely accepted, but paraphrasing the psalms as Watts did was seen to be playing fast and loose with divinely ordained songs. Hence, later in the century, William Romaine wrote of Watts:

> As for his psalms they are so far from the mind of the Spirit, that I am sure if David was to read them, he would not know any one of them to be his. ... The Scripture wants no mending, nay, it is always worse for mending.[3]

Despite such criticism though, these two books completely revolutionized the praise of the church.

Watts' concerns

Watts' criticism of the praise of his day can be seen in the following quote:

> To see the dull indifference, the negligent and the thoughtless air that sits upon the faces of a whole assembly, while the psalm is on their lips, might tempt even a charitable observer to suspect the fervency of inward religion; and 'tis much to be feared that the minds of most of the worshippers are absent or unconcerned.[4]

There are two key aspects which Watts highlights here. He questions both the 'fervency' of singing and the 'mind' of the worshipper. People don't know what they are saying, and they certainly don't feel anything about it. Their singing is both mindless and heartless!

Watts argues that the key fault lies in the content of what was being sung. He said: 'I have been long convinced that one great occasion of this evil arises from the matter and words to which we confine all our songs.' That is, the 'occasion of this evil' was the limitation of singing only these metrical versions of the psalms. Some, he said, were

---

3   William Romaine, *An Essay on Psalmody* (London: 1775), p. 137.

4   Watts, *Works*, 'Hymns', Volume 4, p. 147.

'almost opposite the spirit of the gospel; many of them foreign to the state of the New Testament, and widely different from the present circumstances of Christians.'[5] In other words, the problem is that if the church sings only psalms, we are singing songs that were given under the old covenant. They were given by God and so they were perfect for that moment in salvation history, but that is not the church's moment.

Watts' answer was to provide hymns that were gospel-focused and which expressed the thoughts and feelings of the Christians who were singing. This is what led to his two hymn books. He wanted hymns that spoke explicitly of Jesus, his cross and resurrection; hymns that spoke about forgiveness of sin and renewal by the Holy Spirit; hymns that spoke of the fellowship of the church; hymns that looked forward to Jesus' return and the new creation. He wanted hymns that focused the mind of the Christian on the gospel and allowed expression of the heart of the Christian about the gospel.

This meant, he argued, that we should be allowed to compose new hymns which spoke about Jesus and Christian experience. But second, he argued that the psalms must be paraphrased so as to allow mention of gospel truth (such as naming Jesus) and to reflect the experience of the Christian rather than that of the psalmist. We'll think more about this second argument in a moment.

Revolutionizing the Psalms

In his psalms, then, Watts 'updated' the original words by applying them to Jesus or to the Christian life. He explains his revolutionary approach as follows:

> Where the psalmist uses sharp invectives against his personal enemies, I have endeavoured to turn the edge of them against our spiritual adversaries, sin, Satan, and temptation. ... Where the original runs in the form of a prophecy concerning Christ and his salvation, I have given an historical turn to the sense... When the writers of

---

5   Ibid.

the New Testament have cited or alluded to any part of the psalms, I have often indulged the liberty of a paraphrase, according to the words of Christ, or his apostles...Where the psalmist describes religion by the fear of God, I have often joined faith and love to it: Where he speaks of the pardon of sin, through the mercies of God, I have added the blood and merits of a Saviour... When he attends the ark with shouting into Zion, I sing the ascension of my Saviour into heaven, or his presence in his church on earth...[6]

Watts states that his grand design was to make David 'speak as a Christian'. As we've seen, he was accused of trying to improve on David's inspired writing. But Watts countered: 'The royal author is most honoured when he is made most intelligible' and when his words are rendered in a way that gives 'light and joy to the saints who live two thousand years after him'.

It should be said that sometimes Watts speaks as if Old Testament religion is very different and inferior to that of the New Testament, and I would say he is sometimes too negative over the content of the Psalms as a result. However, he was surely right in wanting to see how the themes in the Psalms were fulfilled in the New Testament and to be able to sing of that fulfilment.

We can see his approach with some examples. First, there are psalms which are explicitly quoted in the New Testament as being about Jesus. For example, in Psalm 16, David speaks about his body not being abandoned to the grave. One of the well-known metrical psalms on this psalm ran like this:

Therefore my heart all grief defies,
my glory does rejoice;
My flesh shall rest in hope to rise,
waked by his pow'rful voice.

Thou, Lord, when I resign my breath,
my soul from hell shall free;
Nor let thy Holy One in death
the least corruption see.

---

6   Ibid., 'Psalms', Volume 4, pp. xvi-xvii.

Thou shall the paths of life display,
that to thy presence lead;
Where pleasures dwell without allay,
and joys that never fade.

However, Peter tells us in Acts that this psalm is a prophecy about Jesus (Acts 2:25-31). So Watts wrote one of his versions like this:

My spirit, Lord, thou wilt not leave
Where souls departed are;
Nor quit my body to the grave,
To see corruption there.

Thou wilt reveal the path of life,
And raise me to thy throne;
Thy courts immortal pleasure give,
Thy presence joys unknown.

Thus, in the name of Christ, the Lord,
The holy David sung;
And Providence fulfils the word
Of his prophetic tongue.

Jesus, whom ev'ry saint adores,
Was crucified and slain:
Behold, the tomb its prey restores!
Behold, he lives again!

Other Psalms were not quoted in the New Testament as being about Jesus, but the themes in them were still fulfilled in Jesus. For example, Psalm 72 is a prayer for the reign of Solomon as king of Israel. So, the standard metrical psalm began like this:

Lord, let thy just decrees the king
in all his ways direct;
And let his son, throughout his reign,
thy righteous laws respect.

And it went on later:

His uncontrolled dominion shall
from sea to sea extend,

Begin at proud Euphrates' streams,
at nature's limits end.

The role of king in the Old Testament, of course, is fulfilled
in Jesus, exalted as God's king, to whom everyone will bow.
So, Watts knew that, instead of a prayer for Solomon, this
psalm should be sung about Jesus. This led him to write
one of his best-known hymns:

Jesus shall reign where'er the sun
Does his successive journeys run;
His kingdom stretch from shore to shore,
Till moons shall wax and wane no more.

A last example is from Psalm 136. This psalm speaks
about God's great acts in history, especially His rescue of
His people from Egypt through the Passover. The standard
metrical psalm had verses about the death of the firstborn
sons in Egypt and the destruction of Israel's enemies in
the Red Sea. Watts' hymn had verses describing these
events from the psalm too, but he couldn't leave things
there. These events point forward to our salvation and
the victory over our enemies through the cross. So, a later
verse of Watts' says this:

He sent his only Son
To save us from our woe,
From Satan, sin, and death,
And every hurtful foe.

Watts argued that in making these jumps to Jesus he
was not really being that radical. After all, he said, this is
exactly what is done in sermons on the Psalms and also in
commentaries. Watts wasn't actually the first to do this
either, but no one had done it as fully nor as well.

It should be added here that some of Watts' paraphrasing
of the psalms revealed a nationalistic streak: he applied
psalms to Britain or her sovereign. For example, Psalm 75
was given the title 'Power and government from God
alone', as it speaks about how God brings down one ruler
and lifts up another. Watts applied this to the ascension

of King William and the 'Glorious Revolution' of 1688, which brought an end to the persecution of dissenters. One verse reads:

> Britain was doomed to be slave,
> Her frame dissolved, her fears were great,
> When God a new supporter gave,
> To bear the pillars of the state.

This was a completely normal way to apply the Bible in Watts' day, so he wasn't doing anything unusual. Today, though, we would be much more wary of applying the Psalms to national events in our own country.

Know what you are singing

There were a couple of key guiding principles behind Watts' hymn-writing. We've touched on them already: they were the mind and the heart of the worshipper. It is worth considering each of these in turn. In doing so, we will understand Watts' view of praise and so why he wrote his hymns the way he did.

Watts was desperately concerned that people understood what they were singing in praise. That might seem obvious to us, but it was far less obvious when he was writing. The church had come through a long period of formal liturgy during which there was much more concern that the right thing was said and done, than whether anyone understood it. Watts, though, said that worshippers must 'obey the direction of the word of God, and sing his praises with understanding'. This meant that he expended a great deal of effort in helping worshippers understand.

First, there was the content of what is sung: Watts says he steered clear of the more obscure and controversial parts of the Christian faith specifically to aid comprehension. Secondly, he avoided poetic turns of phrase that would be beyond the understanding of the man in the street. He also made sure his metaphors were at the level of common speech. This is significant because Watts was a very good poet, but he deliberately avoided poetry that was too 'highbrow', or so clever that people wouldn't follow it easily. So, he said:

I have aimed at ease of numbers and smoothness of sound, and endeavoured to make the sense plain and obvious. If the verse appears so gentle and flowing as to incur the censure of feebleness, I may honestly affirm that sometimes it cost me labour to make it so: some of the beauties of poetry are neglected, and some wilfully defaced; I have thrown out the lines that were too sonorous, and have given an allay to the verse, lest a more exalted turn of thought or language should darken or disturb the devotion of the weakest souls.[7]

Lowering the level you wrote at to accommodate people like this was called the 'art of sinking'. So Watts gladly speaks of his aim to 'sink every line to the level of a whole congregation'. He knew he wouldn't win any prizes for poetry in his hymns as a result, but thought understanding was much more important.

Thirdly, Watts accommodated himself to the current method of singing. This involved a leader reading out a line of a hymn and then the congregation singing it back; then the next line would be read, and so on. This was called 'lining out' a hymn, and was done because people didn't have hymn books; and many people couldn't read anyway. Watts disliked this way of singing because it interrupted the flow of a hymn, but he accepted that it was here to stay for a while. The result was that he made each line contain a complete thought in itself. You can see the difference by comparing Watts' hymns with those from later eras. The later hymns often require reading to the end of a verse before the first line makes any sense, but Watts knew that with the lining-out method, people would lose track of what they were saying if each line didn't stand on its own. This style of writing means that today his hymns have a concise, punchy feel to them.

We also see Watts' desire for understanding in his focus on clear ideas. We previously noted how Watts was concerned that singers knew what the words meant, that each word was connected with a clear and distinct idea.

7   Ibid., 'Hymns', Volume 4, p. 149.

Watts' hymns express this in practice. He focuses each of his hymns on a particular theme. For his psalms, this often meant dividing the psalm into sections with a hymn for each, or, in the case of longer psalms, writing hymns based on certain themes within it. He then presented his theme in clear and simple language. This is usually connected with strong visual imagery which presents the truth to be sung in vivid pictures. Here are a couple of examples: look for how a complex idea is presented in simple, clear and visual ways.

On heaven:

> There is a land of pure delight,
> Where saints immortal reign;
> Infinite day excludes the night,
> And pleasures banish pain.

> There everlasting spring abides,
> And never-with'ring flow'rs:
> Death, like a narrow sea, divides
> This heav'nly land from ours.[8]

On Jesus' death:

> Alas and did my Saviour bleed
> And did my Sovereign die?
> Did he devote that sacred head
> For such a worm as I?

> Was it for crimes that I had done
> He groaned upon the tree?
> Amazing pity! grace unknown!
> And love beyond degree!

> Well might the sun in darkness hide
> And shut his glories in,
> When Christ, the mighty Maker died,
> For man the creature's sin.

---

8   Ibid., 'Hymns', Volume 4, p. 222. On Watts' technique in this hymn see Stephen Marini, 'Hymnody as History: Early Evangelical Hymns and the Recovery of American Popular Religion,' *Church History* 71, no. 2 (2002): p. 300.

Thus might I hide my blushing face
While His dear cross appears,
Dissolve my heart in thankfulness,
And melt my eyes to tears.

Watts' hymns also show a strong sense of logic (as you might expect from a man who wrote a textbook on logic). We see this in the way he orders his material – for example, introducing general terms first and specifics second. This also means that he often begins a hymn with truth about God or Jesus or us, and then later moves to how we should feel and what we should do. So, he moves from content, to feeling, to action. The order is not always that strict – some hymns begin with feelings, for example – but the logical connection is still made.

Watts' communion hymns provide particularly good examples of this. One of them begins like this:

Jesus invites his saints
To meet around his board;
Here pardoned rebels sit and hold
Communion with their Lord.

Here, Watts presents Jesus' words of invitation to the worshipper along with the reminder of their position as pardoned rebels. The hymn continues with a description of Jesus' body and blood nourishing believers, moves to the unity of the body of Christ and finishes with the cry:

Let all our power be joined,
His glorious name to raise;
Pleasure and love fill ev'ry mind,
And ev'ry voice be praise.[9]

So, the truth that the Lord's Supper represents is presented first and then the passionate response follows.

Feel what you are singing
As well as the mind of the worshippers, Watts is also concerned about their hearts. He sees praise as the moment

---

9   Watts, *Works*, 'Hymns', Volume 4, pp. 257-8.

that we speak to God from the heart, and so a variety of emotions should be involved. Watts says about singing in worship:

> The first and chief intent of this part of worship is to express unto God what sense and apprehensions we have of his essential glories; and what notice we take of his works of wisdom and power, vengeance and mercy; it is to vent the inward devotion of our spirits in words of melody, to speak our own experience of divine things, especially our religious joy.[10]

Notice the importance of being able to 'vent the inward devotion of our spirits'. In other words, in singing, we should be helped to express what we feel inside. This is where a comparison is helpful. Watts shows how singing truth about God is different than reading truth about God:

> By reading we are instructed what have been the dealings of God with men in all ages … but songs are generally expressions of our own experiences, or of his glories; we acquaint him what sense we have of his greatness and goodness, and that chiefly in those instances which have some relation to us: we breathe out our souls towards him, and make addresses of praise and acknowledgement to him.[11]

This is tied to Watts' understanding of the purpose of music and singing anything:

> Let us remember that the very power of singing was given to human nature chiefly for this purpose, that our own warmest affections of soul might break out into natural or divine melody, and that the tongue of the worshipper might express his own heart.[12]

For Watts then, our singing should be an overflow of our own experience of God. More than anything else, this is what lies behind Watts' attempts to revolutionize

---

10   Ibid., 'Psalmody', Volume 4, p. 282.

11   Ibid., 'Psalmody', Volume 4, p. 277.

12   Ibid., 'Psalms', Volume 4, p. xiv.

the hymn-singing of his day. He explains that in singing only psalms, this heartfelt devotion of the worshipper is restricted:

> Hence it comes to pass that when spiritual affections are excited within us, and our souls are raised a little above this earth in the beginning of a psalm, we are checked on a sudden in our ascent toward heaven by some expressions that are more suited to the days of carnal ordinances, and fit only to be sung in the worldly sanctuary. When we are just entering into an evangelic frame by some of the glories of the gospel presented in the brightest figures of *Judaism*, yet the very next line perhaps which the clerk parcels out unto us, hath something in it so extremely *Jewish* and cloudy, that darkens our sight of God the saviour: Thus by keeping too close to *David* in the house of God, the veil of *Moses* is thrown over our hearts.[13]

Do you see the argument? If we can sing only psalms, we cannot express our experience of God. We may know moments of heart expression, but before long the words no longer capture our experience of Jesus, and the result is that our souls are 'discomposed', the 'strings of harmony are untuned' and we can only sing with 'cold devotion'.

Watts says his desire is to 'remove this great inconvenience' and so to 'introduce warm devotion into this part of divine worship'. In providing appropriate lyrics which speak about Christian experience, Watts is solving this problem. He says of his hymns:

> The most frequent tempers and changes of our spirit, and conditions of our life, are here copied, and the breathings of our piety expressed according to the variety of our passions; our love, our fear, our hope, our desire, our sorrow, our wonder and our joy.[14]

This concern for praise that is offered with our hearts as well as our minds led Watts to write his hymns in a certain way. We saw in an earlier chapter that Watts thought we

---

13   Ibid., 'Hymns', Volume 4, p. 147.

14   Ibid., 'Hymns', Volume 4, p. 148.

should meditate on gospel truth to raise our passions or emotions. He believed that that can happen in times of praise as well as in personal reflection. So, he said that praise involves warming our hearts 'by the meditations of the loving kindness of God, and the multitude of his tender mercies'.

So, Watts writes hymns which give the clear and dramatic portrayal of Christian truth in terms we can understand (as we saw above), and then leads us on to express how we feel about that truth. For example, a hymn describing Christ dying because of our sins ends like this:

> Whilst with a melting, broken heart,
> My murdered Lord I view,
> I'll raise revenge against my sins,
> And slay the murderers too.[15]

In choosing emotional words to be sung, a hymn writer is effectively telling us what we should feel as we sing. Watts was perfectly happy to do this. So, in the verse above, he is telling us that as we consider Jesus' death we should have a 'melting' and a 'broken' heart, and should be inspired to put to death our sin which was the cause of Jesus' death.

It is sometimes said that Watts' hymns are full of objective truth about God and the gospel (which is true), while other hymns writers, such as Charles Wesley, include lots of emotion (which is also true). While there is a grain of truth here, what is wrong about this observation is that it misses the amount of emotion in Watts (and for that matter, the amount of truth in Wesley). Here are some examples from different hymns; look at how Watts is guiding us in what we should feel or how we should sing:

> Such wond'rous love awakes the lip
> Of saints that were almost asleep,
> To speak the praises of thy name,
> And makes our cold affections flame.

> My heart grows warm with holy fire,
> And kindles with a pure desire:

---

15   Ibid., 'Hymns', Volume 4, p. 236.

Come, my dear *Jesus*, from above,
And feed my soul with heavenly love.

Now shall my inward joys arise,
And burst into a song;
Almighty love inspires my heart,
And pleasure tunes my tongue.

'Twere you that pulled the vengeance down
Upon his guiltless head:
Break, break, my heart! O burst mine eyes!
And let my sorrows bleed.

O! What immortal joys I felt,
And raptures all divine,
When *Jesus* told me, I was his,
And my Beloved mine!

The effect that Watts wanted to see when people were singing is illustrated in a letter from his friend Philip Doddridge. Doddridge writes to Watts describing an occasion singing one of Watts' hymns and says:

> ... and in that part of the worship I had the satisfaction to observe tears in the eyes of several of the auditory, and after the service was over some of them told me that they were not able to sing, so deeply were their minds affected with it ...[16]

In this picture of heartfelt, responsive praise to God, Watts sees times of singing as the nearest the church gets to the heavenly state:

> While we sing the praises of our God in his church, we are employed in that part of worship which of all others is the nearest a-kin to heaven ...[17]

> Praise is the sweetest part of divine worship; it is a short heaven here on earth.[18]

---

16 ———, *The Posthumous Works of the Late Learned and Reverend Isaac Watts, D.D. In two volumes. Compiled from papers in possession of his immediate successors: adjusted and published by a gentleman of the University of Cambridge* (London: T. Becket and J. Bew, 1779), Volume 2, pp. 26-7.

17 ———, *Works*, 'Hymns', Volume 4, p. 147.

18 Ibid., 'Remnants', Volume 4, p. 628.

This concern for heartfelt devotion in praise means Watts wanted his hymn writing to come from his heart in the first place. He wanted his lyrics to be an expression of genuine Christian experience which he felt himself. So, Watts says about writing poetry in general:

> If the heart were first inflamed from heaven, and the meditation were not left alone to form the devotion, and pursue a cold scent, but only called in as an assistant to the worship, then the song would end when the inspiration ceases; the whole composure would be of a piece, all meridian light and meridian fervour; and the same pious flame would be propagated, and kept glowing in the heart of him that reads.[19]

This is a good summary of Watts' ideal hymn: high points of light (understanding) and fervour (emotion), coming from the warmed heart of the writer, and resulting in the same in the singer.

Watts knew, though, that in order for this to happen we needed far more than good lyrics and good music. You may remember that when we looked at his writings on heart religion he spoke about the need for the work of the Spirit. He knew that the Spirit had to take the truth and impress it on us for us to feel rightly, and the Spirit was Himself the source of right feelings as much as of right understanding. Watts knew this must happen in singing as in every other area.

We see this in some of his hymns themselves. For example, a hymn entitled 'Breathing after the holy Spirit; or Fervency of Devotion desired' speaks of the emptiness of passionless praise:

> In vain we tune our formal songs,
> In vain we strive to rise;
> *Hosannas* languish on our tongues,
> And our devotion dies.

It proceeds to intercede for the work of the Spirit to transform this state:

---

19 Ibid., 'Horae Lyricae', Volume 4, p. 323.

Come Holy Spirit, heav'nly Dove,
With all thy quick'ning powers;
Come, shed abroad a Saviour's love,
And that shall kindle ours.[20]

Conclusion

The greatest lasting impact Isaac Watts had was on reforming the praise of the church. This was because he saw that Christians needed to be able to sing of the gospel of Jesus Christ and of their experience of the blessings of that gospel. So he argued for composing new hymns and for 'updating' the psalms. It was also because he saw the need to link people's understanding and their emotions; he wrote hymns which presented clear ideas to their heads and drew them to express their hearts. It was also, of course, because he was a very good poet, and so wrote great lyrics which captured both truth and feeling.

Let's see that in what is probably Watts' best-known hymn (here with an original verse which is often left out of modern versions):

When I survey the wondrous cross
On which the Prince of glory died,
My richest gain I count but loss,
And pour contempt on all my pride.

Forbid it, Lord, that I should boast,
Save in the death of Christ my God!
All the vain things that charm me most,
I sacrifice them to His blood.

See from His head, His hands, His feet,
Sorrow and love flow mingled down!
Did e'er such love and sorrow meet,
Or thorns compose so rich a crown?

His dying crimson, like a robe,
Spreads o'er His body on the tree;
Then I am dead to all the globe,
And all the globe is dead to me.

---

20   Ibid., 'Hymns', Volume 4, p. 211.

Were the whole realm of nature mine,
That were an offering far too small;
Love so amazing, so divine,
Demands my soul, my life, my all.

Watts longed to see the church praising God for the wonder of the gospel and so giving glory to God and being built up in the faith:

O may I live to see such psalmody performed in these evangelic beauties of holiness... Then my soul shall be all admiration, my tongue shall humbly attempt to mingle in the worship, and assist the harmony and the joy.[21]

What should we learn from Watts about praise?

We should learn that the talents of great poets can be used for the good of the church; but they should be prepared not to be seen as the greatest poets, but rather write in a way which serves the people singing.

We should learn that the psalms are a great model for our praise. While we might not sing psalms as they stand, they should surely inspire more songs than they do and act as a shaping influence on our praise.

We should learn the importance of understanding what we sing and so engaging our minds in the content of what we are singing.

We should learn the importance of feeling what we sing and so engaging our hearts in the appropriate affections for what we are singing.

We should learn that for all this to happen we need the work of the Spirit.

---

21   Ibid., 'Psalmody', Volume 4, p. 281.

9
FACING SUFFERING

We've seen Watts' poor health in previous chapters. His illness meant that he had a complete absence from ministry for four years from 1712 to 1716. After that, his health fluctuated a great deal, resulting in an ongoing but limited ministry. He lived with the Abney family just outside London and travelled in to church whenever he was able to. This remained the pattern for the rest of his life.

In this chapter, we will pause and consider how Watts dealt with such an ongoing and debilitating condition.

Poetic descriptions
In an earlier chapter we read some of Watts' poetry about his illness. That was only a brief excerpt! He wrote several long poems, especially in the painful years of 1712-13. This group of poems is entitled 'Thoughts and Meditations in a Long Sickness'. We'll look at some of what he wrote. Can I encourage you to read these slowly? I have rarely appreciated poetry and would tend to skip over it in books, but have come to really appreciate these.[1]

The first poem describes something of Watts' experience, probably of hallucinations, where his illness is likened to being thrown around on the sea.

My frame of nature is a ruffled sea,
And my disease the tempest. Nature feels

---

1   All these poems are found in ibid., 'Horae Lyricae', Volume 4, p. 524ff.

A strange commotion to her inmost centre;
The throne of reason shakes. 'Be still my thoughts;
Peace and be still.' In vain my reason gives
The peaceful word; my spirit strives in vain
To calm the tumult, and command my thoughts.
This flesh, this circling blood, these brutal powers,
Made to obey, turn rebels to the mind,
Nor hear its laws. The engine rules the man.
Unhappy change! When nature's meaner springs,
Fired to impetuous ferments, break all order;
When little restless atoms rise and reign
Tyrants in sovereign uproar, and impose
Ideas of the mind; confused ideas
Of non-existents and impossibles,
Who can describe them? Fragments of old dreams,
Borrowed from midnight, torn from fairy fields
And fairy skies, and regions of the dead,
Abrupt, ill-sorted. O 'tis all confusion!

Watts eloquently describes the feeling of his body overthrowing his mind. The result is distress and confusion. He is rendered helpless. Clearly, this was terribly disturbing. What we should note is Watts' willingness to *describe* such a disturbing experience. It is all too easy for Christians to pretend everything is OK when it's not, or that they are OK when they are not. Watts carefully described how out of control he felt.

The next poem in Watts' collection, though, expresses his confidence in God through his illness, especially the confidence of feeling secure in forgiveness:

Yet, gracious God amidst these storms of nature,
Thine eyes behold a sweet and sacred calm
Reign through the realms of conscience: all within
Lies peaceful and composed. 'Tis wondrous grace
Keeps off thy terrors from this humble bosom,
Though stained with sins and follies, yet serene
In penitential peace and cheerful hope;
Sprinkled and guarded with atoning blood.
Thy vital smiles amidst this devastation,
Like heavenly sunbeams hid behind the clouds,
Break out in happy moments with bright radiance,

Cleaving the gloom; the fair celestial light
Softens and gilds the horrors of the storm,
And richest cordials to the heart conveys.
O glorious solace of immense distress,
A conscience and a God! A friend at home
And a better Friend on high! This is my Rock
Of firm support, my Shield of sure defence
Against infernal arrows. Rise, my soul,
Put on thy courage: Here's the living spring
Of joys divinely sweet and ever new,
'A peaceful conscience and a smiling heaven.'

What a wonderful comfort to hold on to! A 'glorious solace'. This is a great thing to pray for yourself and others in dark days. He goes on:

Weak as my zeal is, yet my zeal is true;
It bears the trying furnace. Love divine
Constrains me; I am thine. Incarnate love
Has seized and holds me in almighty arms:
Here's my salvation, my eternal hope.
Amidst the wreck of worlds and dying nature,
'I am the Lord's, and he forever mine.'

Again, there is the confidence that God has taken hold of him. At a time when he feels thrown around in chaos, that is great comfort.

Within these poems there is not only the reassurance of belonging to God; there is also the expression of trust and confidence in Him. One of the greatest challenges for the Christian who is suffering is that he or she continues to trust that God is sovereign, and so in control, and also that God is loving, and so is achieving His good purpose.

Watts' poems contain these elements. He reminds himself both of God's sovereign power, and that He showed His love in the cross. So, Watts says out loud that God is sovereign over his illness, and that He cares for him in his illness. For example, in one poem Watts speaks about wanting to make time go faster to speed him through the slow-moving agony of illness and on to recovery. And then he says:

Ah foolish ravings of a fruitless wish
And spirit too impatient! Knowest thou not,
My soul, the power that made thee? He alone
Who formed the spheres, rolls them in destined rounds
Unchangeable. Adore, and trust, and fear him:
He is the Lord of life. Address his throne,
And wait before his foot, with awesome hope
Submissive.

This perspective allowed Watts to make remarks such as this one about his illness: 'I know not but my days of restraint and confinement by affliction may appear my brightest days, when I come to take a review of them in the light of heaven.'[2]

Christians have often struggled to express God's goodness and sovereignty and still to speak about how terrible their suffering is. But this is the Biblical model – to hold on to God *and* to say how much it hurts. This is what we see in the psalms very clearly, and Watts echoes the cry of the psalmist, asking, 'How long?' He speaks of the day of rest, Sunday, coming, with God's work and worship, but how his illness prevents him from taking part:

Sweet day of rest, devote to God and heaven,
And heavenly business, purposes divine,
Angelic work; but not to me returns
Rest with the day. Ten thousand hurrying thoughts
Bear me away tumultuous far from heaven
And heavenly work. In vain I heave, and toil,
Overpowered and vanquished still: they drag me down
From things celestial, and confine my sense
To present maladies. Unhappy state,
Where the poor spirit is subdued to endure
Unholy idleness, a painful absence
And bound to bear the agonies and woes
From God, and heaven, and angels' blessed work,
That sickly flesh on shattered nerves imposes.
How long, O Lord, how long?

Wonderfully, Watts also knew times of recovery and wrote a poem of praise as well:

---

2   Milner, *Watts*, p. 302.

Happy for man, that the slow circling moons
And long revolving seasons measure out
The tiresome pains of nature! Present woes
Have their sweet ends. Ease and cheerful health
With slow approach (so providence ordains)
Revisit their forsaken mansion here,
And days of useful life diffuse their dawn
O'er the dark cottage of my weary soul.
My vital powers resume their vigour now,
My spirit feels her freedom, shakes her wings,
Exults and wanders o'er a thousand scenes,
Surveys the world, and with full stretch of thought
Grasps her ideas; while impatient zeal
Awakens my tongue to praise.

Even in his praise for healing he reminds us of the need to
bow before God's unknown purposes in our suffering and
trust Him:

Almighty power, I love thee, blissful Name,
My Healer God: and may my inmost heart
Love and adore forever! O 'tis good
To wait submissive at thy holy throne,
To leave petitions at thy feet, and bear,
Thy frowns and silence with a patient soul.
The hand of mercy is not too short to save,
Nor is the ear of heavenly pity deaf
To mortal cries. It noticed all my groans,
And sighs, and long complaints, with wise delay,
Tho' painful to the sufferer, and thy hand
In proper moment brought desired relief.

There is much to learn here. We are far less likely to speak
of God's 'wise delay' when we are suffering. We need to
learn, as did Watts, to leave our requests with God and
'wait submissive at thy holy throne.'

Letters of sorrow

During his times of illness, Watts communicated with his
congregation regularly by letter. In these we see several
things. We gain another angle on how Watts viewed his
illness; we see the loving relationship between him and his

congregation; and we see an example of the tensions in relationships that can be brought about by such separation.

It is many people's experience that times of suffering are times they have learnt more about themselves than any other. Watts certainly found this to be the case. He said, 'Long afflictions are soul-searching providences, and reveal the secrets of the heart and omissions of duty that were unobserved in a day of peace.' This is one way God uses suffering: it holds a mirror up to our hearts and forces us to look into it, in a way that would never happen if life were easy.

Expressing this principle, Watts wrote to his congregation in 1713:

> I bow to his wisdom and holiness, and am learning obedience by the things that I suffer, and many lessons of righteousness and grace which I hope hereafter to publish amongst you.[3]

Later, he wrote:

> While I cry out with David under confinement, 'When shall I come and appear before God?' I am not very solicitous whether I make my appearance in the church below or in that above. I should be glad to serve my Lord Jesus among you again if he saw fit, and to tell you from long experience what words of grace I have lived upon, what promises have been my support, and what need I have of divine assistance hourly to bear up my spirits under so sore and heavy a burden.[4]

We mentioned above the need to hold on to God's sovereignty and His goodness. We saw that expressed in Watts' poems; we see it too in his letters. He poignantly says, 'God's heart has love in it while his hand gives us conscious pain.'

Perhaps one of the most crucial steps in enduring suffering is that of 'acceptance'. We can bear with suffering for a while, always looking forward to its end. That can

---

3   Watts, 'Wattiana,' 4 Nov 1713, p. 58.
4   Ibid., 6 Aug 1715, p. 78.

be the thought which gives us encouragement and hope –
we live for the time it will be gone. Of course, we should
look forward to its end (it would be odd not to), but our
hope must ultimately be in God, not in recovery. So, what
is desperately difficult, but desperately needed, is that we
accept our suffering from God's hand. We need to bow the
knee before God in our suffering. Watts once said during
a period of illness:

> The business of a Christian is to bear the will of God, as
> well as to do it. If I were in health, I could be doing *that*,
> and *that* I may do now.[5]

Elsewhere, Watts teaches others about the lessons he has
learnt in terms of 'resignation':

> If I had learnt the duty of resignation myself I would
> attempt to teach it you, and say there is nothing that
> gives the soul such a sweet calm and composure under
> the sharpest sorrows as perpetual contemplation of the
> wisdom and goodness and sovereignty of God as our God,
> and a humble submission to his will in all things.[6]

Such acceptance, although hard, is the source of peace.
Such acceptance means we can look beyond our struggles
to God's purposes, in us and elsewhere. Watts is thus able
to write these words:

> Blessed is his name who hath thus far supported me;
> I long to serve him, and I think I value my life for no
> other purpose; but he wants me not, nor my poor services;
> and however he deals with me I join heartily with all your
> prayers for spiritual and eternal welfare of this church to
> which I am engaged in all the bonds of love, gratitude and
> the gospel.[7]

Watts also knew the support and encouragement of his
congregation. His letters give thanks for their prayers,

---

5   Jennings, *A Funeral Sermon for the Late Reverend Isaac Watts D.D.*, p. 34.
6   Watts, 'Wattiana,' 14 Apr 1716, p. 81.
7   Ibid., 12 Feb 1718, p. 100.

support and patience. He, in turn, rejoiced to hear good news of how they were growing:

> I rejoice to hear of your union, your love, your attendance on the worship of the church. This has been a great comfort to my thoughts in the time of my affliction and absence.[8]

There were times when the reports back on the church included disturbances of some kind. This led him to give instruction and encouragement:

> And now Brethren dearly beloved, I entreat you by the love of Christ to you and the love you bear to Christ our common Lord, that there be no contentions among you... Let every thing that is debated be with great calmness and so much the more in my absence; each of you believing concerning one another that you sincerely seek the honour of Christ and union and peace of the church, as I believe concerning you all.[9]

It was Watts' absences because of illness that led the church to appoint Samuel Price as assistant and then co-pastor. Watts often comments on his colleague, supporting him in the eyes of the congregation and assuring them that he is behind him:

> Look upon him therefore as a part of me that is present with you; look upon me as the absent part of him. For I trust we have one heart and a single eye in all our work.[10]

There were times, however, when Watts' illness and absence led to real tension between him and his congregation. Given how long his illness was, and how frequently it returned, this was perhaps inevitable. Watts was living at this time with the Abney family, and he occasionally preached for them on a Sunday evening. When the congregation heard about this, though, it raised the inevitable question: why does he not preach to us, rather than to them?

---

8   Ibid., 4 Nov 1713, p. 58.

9   Ibid.

10   Ibid., 3 Ap 1714, p. 69.

One letter exists where he broaches this issue. He says that his times of strength are so infrequent and uncertain that he does not know when he will be able to do anything. He also assures them that the Abney family sees the church as the key priority. So, he says, 'I would not give you any suspicion that I deprive you of my strength by employing it in another way.' But, though he wrote this letter, Watts did not send it to the congregation, presumably feeling it might open a can of worms that would cause more trouble.

That was in 1716, and the need to defend himself reoccurred. In 1718, he did send these words to the church:

> He that sees the secrets of all hearts knows the inward longing and desires I felt toward this assembly; but he that gave me this inclination is a witness of my incapacity. I wait His time and seek and pray for submission and length of patience.[11]

During the four-year period that Watts was absent, he did ask the church to stop paying his salary, but they refused. They later also gave him additional funds to help pay for doctors' bills.

Writing for his people

Watts' later periods of absence led him to write some of his works; he sometimes had enough energy to write but not to pastor in person. He also wrote in order to provide contact with and help to his congregation. In light of this, many of his works were written for them and address his illness and absence directly. We see this in his first volume of sermons (published in 1721), which addressed his congregation in the preface:

> While I was thus walking among you in the fellowship of the gospel with mutual delight, God was pleased to weaken my strength in the way, and thereby has given you fairer opportunity to show the vigour of your affection under my long weakness and confinement. Your diligence and zeal in maintaining public worship in the church,

---

11   Ibid., 12 Feb 1718, p. 100.

under the pastoral care of my dear brother and colleague, your special days and hours of prayer for my recovery, your constant and fervent addresses to the throne of grace on my account in your weekly solemn assemblies, and your cheerful supply of my necessities under so tedious an affliction, have made me your debtor in a high degree, and have strengthened the bonds of my duty, by adding to them the bonds of your love.[12]

Watts may be putting a shine on things here, but there was clearly great mutual affection between him and the congregation. Although he was at this point back from his four years of absence and preaching with some regularity, we can also still see the need to give reassurance:

As fast as my health increases, you may assure yourselves it is devoted to your edification. It often grieves me to think how poor, feeble and short, are my present labours among you; and yet what days of faintness I generally feel after every such attempt; so that I am continually prevented in my design of successive visits to you... I bless God heartily, and you are my witnesses, that in my better seasons of health heretofore, and in the intervals of my studies, I was not a stranger to your private families, nor thoughtless to your souls' improvement.

His times of absence, though, meant he wanted to write down some sermons so that he could continue to have some influence and helpful ministry among his people:

What shall I do now to make up these defects? What can I do more pleasing and profitable to you, than to seize the advantages of my retirement, to review some of those discourses which have assisted your faith and joy in my former ministry, and to put them into your hands? Thus something of me shall abide with you in your several houses, while I am incapable of much public labour, and of personal visits.

Years later he wrote his book of catechisms for children, which we have already examined. This is another example

---

12 ———, *Works*, 'Sermons', Volume 1, p. xx.

of a book written for his church during a period of illness. The preface is written to 'The parents and governors of the families belonging to the congregation which usually assembles for worship at Berry Street, London.' Watts says in that preface:

> While my want of a strong constitution of body, and my necessary retirements from the city, render me incapable of paying so many visits to your families, and promoting their spiritual welfare so much as I would gladly do, I humbly hope this little book may be attended with the divine blessing; that your children may derive from it abundant benefits; that the principles of piety and goodness being early instilled into their minds, they may be better secured against the temptations of infidelity, vice and profaneness; that they may stand up in the following age as supports and ornaments of true religion, and bear up the name of Christ with honour in a degenerate and sinful world.

As we've examined, Watts wrote many hymns, and some of these reflect his experience of suffering. In the Psalms we read both songs of praise and songs of lament, cries of joy and cries of anguish. Both are part of the Christian experience and we need both today. Watts certainly wrote great hymns of triumphant praise, but he also wrote hymns of sorrow. Some of these, like his poems above, were written directly in response to a period of illness. For instance, in 1736, Watts was forced to spend most of the year away from his church due to illness, but during that time he wrote a hymn entitled 'Complaint and hope under great pain'. Here it is:

> LORD, I am pained; but I resign
> My body to thy will;
> Tis grace, 'tis wisdom all divine,
> Appoints the pains I feel.
>
> Dark are the ways of Providence,
> While they who love thee groan:
> Thy reasons lie concealed from sense,
> Mysterious and unknown.

Yet nature may have leave to speak,
And plead before her God,
Lest the o'er-burdened heart should break
Beneath thine heavy rod,

These groans and sighs and flowing tears
Give my poor spirit ease;
While every groan my Father hears,
And every tear he sees.

Is not some smiling hour at hand,
With peace upon its wings?
Give it, O God, thy swift command,
With all the joys it brings.[13]

Notice the themes we've seen already: the submission to God's will, the admission of pain, the request for relief and the reassurance of God's care. These hymns then were sung by Watts' congregation and many, many others, and so his experience of suffering allowed others to express their own pains and sorrows.

Advice to others

In 2 Corinthians 1, the apostle Paul speaks about God as the 'Father of compassion and the God of all comfort who comforts us in all our troubles' (vv. 3-4). In that passage, he goes on to say that God comforts us so that we can comfort others – we can pass on God's comfort. Watts was certainly an example of this.

We see this in his letters. To a minister who was suffering, he wrote:

It is my hearty desire for you, that your faith may ride out the storms of temptation, and the anchor of your hope may hold, being fixed within the veil. There sits Jesus our forerunner, who sailed over this rough sea before us, and has given us a chart, even his word, where the shelves and rocks, the fierce currents and dangers, are well described. And he is our pilot, and will conduct us to the shores of happiness. I am persuaded, that in a future state we shall take a sweet review of those scenes of providence, which have been involved in the thickest darkness, and trace

---

13   Ibid., 'Remnants of time', Volume 4, p. 610.

those footsteps of God where he walked with us through the deepest waters. This will be a surprising delight to survey the manifold harmony of clashing dispensations, and to have those perplexing riddles laid open to the eyes of our souls, and read the full meaning of them in set characters of wisdom and grace.[14]

This is Watts applying to others the lessons he had learned for himself.

Watts also wrote to a lady whose sister was very ill in the following way:

But every place is a soil where the plants of grace may bring forth fruit to God, and where painful dispensations, attending one whom we love, may excite in us some pious meditation.[15]

In other words, God is working for our good in all things (Rom. 8:28). Times of suffering can bring us to our senses and make us realize what is truly important. Watts goes on:

We are too ready to forget our God, our hope, our home, our eternal interest, amidst the flatteries of prosperity and pleasure.

This perspective means he prays for someone to recover that she may return with 'renewed health', but also with an 'improved soul'. It is wise for us, too, to pray that sort of prayer and to look to grow through our troubles in that way.

Perhaps one of the most poignant letters from Watts is to his father, who lay ill and dying.[16] He writes as a son who thought that he himself might die earlier:

'Tis now ten days since I heard from you, and learned by my nephews that you had recovered from a very threatening illness. When you are in danger of life I believe my sister is afraid to let me know the worst for fear of affecting me

14 Milner, *Watts*, pp. 302-3.
15 Watts, 'Wattiana,' Dr Watts to Mrs Richier (3 Dec 1728), p. 145.
16 Gibbons, *Memoirs*, pp. 2-3.

too much. But as I feel old age daily advancing on myself, I am endeavouring to be ready for my removal hence; and though it gives a shock to nature when what has been long dear to one is taken away, yet reason and religion should teach us to expect it in these scenes of mortality, and a dying world. Blessed be God for our immortal hopes through the blood of Jesus, who has taken away the sting of death! What could such dying creatures do without the comforts of the gospel? I hope you feel those satisfactions of soul on the borders of life, which nothing can give but this gospel, which you taught us all in our younger years. May these divine consolations support your spirits, under all your growing infirmities; and may our blessed Saviour form your soul to such a heavenly frame, that you may wait with patience amidst the languors of life, for a joyful passage into the land of immortality! May no cares nor pains ruffle, nor afflict your spirit! May you maintain a constant serenity at heart, and sacred calmness of mind, as one who has long past midnight, and is in view of the dawning day! The night is far spent, the day is at hand. Let the garments of light be found upon us, and let us lift up our heads, for our redemption draws high. Amen.

I am, dear Sir, your most affectionate obedient Son,

Isaac Watts

Living with and learning from suffering

Watts, then, was a great example of how to both live with suffering and learn from it. He reminds us that life can be very painful, and that such pain does not always have an obvious purpose. However, we should and can submit to God in it, cry out to Him, lean on Him and grow through it.

Watts is, of course, best known for his hymns of praise. But he once wrote a meditation on praise in his work *Remnants of Time*, in which he reflects that there have been many times in his life when praise seemed far away. He still speaks of the great joy in praising God for His goodness and mercy, but he knows too well that the Christian life is not only made up of joy and so praise. Rather, he says, there are times when praise is silent to make room for prayers of lament, help and trust:

> God loves prayer as well as praise: His sovereignty is honoured by humble waiting, as well as his goodness by holy gratitude and joy. If praise be silent, then let prayer be more fervent.[17]

---

17   Watts, *Works*, 'Remnants of Time', Volume 4, p. 628.

10

LIVING TO SEE REVIVAL

Earlier in this book we've seen the poor state of religion in England in Watts' day. Watts and many others lamented over this and prayed for God to act. They also acted to try to revive true and vibrant Christianity. Eventually, revival came. God acted in an extraordinary way in what became known as the 'Evangelical Revival' in Britain, and the 'Great Awakening' in New England.

The most prominent person involved in New England was Jonathan Edwards, pastor of a church in the town of Northampton. In the mid-1730s, Edwards' church saw a remarkable work of God. People were brought under great conviction of sin, and then to great assurance of salvation, and on to great zealousness in living for God.

In Britain, George Whitefield and then the Wesley brothers, John and Charles, were the most significant leaders – although many others were involved as well. Huge gatherings of people came to listen to these speakers across the country. Many came to faith or were revived in their faith. Whitefield travelled back and forth across the Atlantic and so was very involved in the revival in New England as well.

Our purpose here is not to tell the story of these revivals themselves – which is a whole other book – but rather to look at Watts' connection with them and his response to them.

Revival in New England

Over the previous years, Watts had developed a network of correspondence with ministers in New England. He was one of England's best-known ministers himself and took a keen interest in the political and spiritual development of Britain's American colony. For example, he gave many theological books to the recently formed Yale College in New Haven – some were his own publications, others were by well-known Puritan writers.

His most frequent correspondence was with Benjamin Colman, a minister in Boston, whom Watts had met when Colman had visited England. Colman and his friendship with Watts were to prove significant in spreading the news of the New England revival.

During 1737, Watts began to hear of the remarkable events in New England. For example, Elisha Williams, the rector of Yale College, wrote to him as follows:

> Since the advancement of Christ's kingdom is always your rejoicing, it will not be disagreeable to you if I should acquaint you that there has been a remarkable revival of religion in several parts of this country, in ten parishes in the county of Hampshire, in the Massachusetts province, where it began a little more than year since, and in near twenty parishes of this colony.[1]

This revival included the advance of the gospel among native Indians. Williams went on:

> This mercy has also reached some of the Indians, especially a tribe of them, to whom Mr Sergeant, lately a tutor at this college, a learned pious man, has gone, and entirely devoted himself to serve the interest of Christ among them, and since last October has baptised fifty infants and adults, of whom he says he has reason to hope they will live worthy of the profession they have made; that they seem surprised at the change they feel in themselves, and compare their former state of heathenism to the darkness of the night, their Christianity to the brightness of the day. These and such like metaphors they use to express the

---

1   Milner, *Watts*, pp. 545-6.

difference between their former and present state. Would to God this blessing might be extended not only through our land and nation but the whole world![2]

Mr Sergeant, the missionary to this Indian tribe, was himself full of admiration and thanks to Watts. He had earlier written about his own debt to Watts:

> I wish I were worthy of the love of so excellent a man as the Rev Dr Watts, whom all the world admires and loves. And if I may be thought to deserve in any measure the opinion of the world, it is not a little owing to the doctor's ingenious writings, which have the force to charm minds to the love of piety and virtue, and infuse something of his own spirit into his readers.[3]

Benjamin Colman also told Watts of the revival and about this work among the Indian population. He informed Watts that his own writings were also of use directly in the work among the Indian population. Watts' catechisms were found to be particularly useful, presumably because they tried to render the fundamentals of the faith in simple terms and easy English. John Sergeant later wrote to Watts, saying, 'Your Catechisms are taught among us, and have learned to speak Indian'.[4]

Watts wrote in response:

> I am much pleased with Mr Sergeant's character and conduct, and give solemn thanks to my God that he has made my writings in any way serviceable toward his qualifications for his work, and that my blessed Saviour is pleased to honour my little Catechisms to teach the rudiments of his gospel to the heathens.[5]

Watts followed this work among the American Indians with great interest and was often updated by various correspondents in New England.

---

2   Ibid., p. 547.
3   Ibid., p. 539.
4   Gibbons, *Memoirs*, p. 439.
5   Watts, 'Letters,' p. 349.

Spreading the news

Having described the revival in outline to Watts, Benjamin Colman later obtained a letter from Jonathan Edwards describing the specific events in Northampton. He sent part of this on to Watts, who was astounded at what he read. Watts wrote back:

> And now I come to Mr Edwards' narrative of the work of God in Northampton and the places round about. I confess, Sir, your first mention of this matter gave me a religious pleasure, and I longed for a more complete account of it; but the extract from the letter which you have made exceeds my expectation and greatly increases my joy. These are certainly little specimens of what Christ and his grace can do when he shall begin to revive his own work and to spread his kingdom through the earth; and if he begins in America, I adore his good pleasure and rejoice, but wait for the blessing in European countries.[6]

This extract reveals something of Watts' expectation of the 'last days'. He believed that God promised that Christ's kingdom would grow and extend across the earth before Jesus Himself returned. That is why he refers to this revival as a 'little specimen' of what Christ will do.

Colman had also sent Edwards' letter to Dr Guyse, another minister and friend of Watts. Guyse and Watts conferred with each other and agreed:

> We are of the opinion that so strange and surprising a work of God that we have not heard of anything like it since the Reformation, nor perhaps since the days of the apostles, should be published...

So followed a flurry of letters between Watts, Colman and Edwards, which resulted in the first account of the revival in New England by Jonathan Edwards being printed in London, with a preface by Watts and Guyse. It was entitled: *A Faithful Narrative of the Surprising Work of God...* (1737).

In this work, Edwards described the recent events at Northampton and the surrounding areas, focusing on the

---

6   Ibid., p. 353.

way in which people came to conviction of sin and the truth of the gospel. It was primarily, he explains, not about new knowledge – as everyone had heard the message of the gospel – but about personal realization of that knowledge:

> The arguments are the same that they have heard hundreds of times; but the force of the arguments, and their conviction by them, is altogether new; they come with a new and before unexperienced power. Before they *heard it* was so, and they *allowed it* to be so; but now they *see it* to be so indeed. Things now look exceedingly plain to them, and they wonder that they did not see them before.[7]

This new conviction was often accompanied by emotion – people felt guilt over their sin and felt joy over salvation. Edwards said:

> It was very wonderful to see after what manner persons' affections were sometimes moved and wrought upon, when God did, as it were, suddenly open their eyes and let into their minds a sense of the greatness of his grace, and fullness of Christ, and his readiness to save, who before were broken with apprehensions of divine wrath, and sunk into an abyss under a sense of guilt...[8]

This meant people often expressed great emotion, as Edwards went on to describe:

> Their joyful surprise has caused their hearts as it were to leap, so that they have been ready to break forth into laughter, tears often at the same time issuing like a flood, and intermingling a loud weeping. And sometimes they haven't been able to forbear crying out with a loud voice expressing their great admiration.[9]

Edwards went on to give in-depth accounts of some individuals and their extraordinary stories of conversion and subsequent closeness to God and experience of God.

---

7   Jonathan Edwards, *A faithful narrative of the conversion of many hundred souls in Northampton. In a letter to Dr. B. Colman, and published with a preface by Dr. Watts and Dr. Guyse* (London, 1737), p. 71.

8   Ibid., p. 59.

9   Ibid., pp. 59-60.

To us this sounds wonderful, but in the eighteenth century it all smacked of 'enthusiasm'. The accusation would be that it was all hysteria and hype, froth and emotion. Edwards himself tried to argue against that accusation in his account. Watts and Guyse knew they were opening themselves up to such accusations by promoting this work. They too tried to guard against it in their preface and to give a semi-apology for some of Edwards' decisions about what to include. But they say:

> Upon the whole, whatever defects any reader may find, or imagine, in this narrative, we are well satisfied that such an eminent work of God ought not to be concealed from the world. And as it was the Rev. Author's opinion, so we declare it to be ours also, that it is very likely that this account of such an extraordinary and illustrious appearance of divine grace in the conversion of sinners, may, by the blessing of God, have a happy effect on the minds of men, towards the honour and enlargement of the kingdom of Christ, much more than any supposed imperfection in this representation of it can do injury.[10]

There has been discussion of whether Watts and Guyse took the liberty of editing Edwards' manuscript so as to tone down some of the most 'enthusiastic' sections. The evidence for this is slight as the American edition of the work (untouched by Watts and Guyse) is virtually identical. However, one letter by Watts suggests something like this happened. Having commented on some factual errors that crept in unintentionally in the printing, Watts continues:

> As for the alterations we made, we were afraid to leave out very much, lest we fall under the same censure that Dr Colman did in his accurate and judicious abridgement; but we both agree that there was not one alteration made which we did not think perfectly agreeable to the sentiments of the writer. It was necessary to make some alterations of the language, lest we together with the book should have been exposed to much more contempt and ridicule on this account, though I may tell my friend that it is not a little of that kind we have both met with.[11]

---

10   Ibid., p. xv.

11   Watts, 'Letters,' p. 360.

We cannot judge exactly what changes were made as the original they were working from no longer exists. But despite the dangers of association, Watts clearly felt this was a work of God and he should promote it and rejoice in it.

The overall position Watts took towards the revivals, then, was decidedly positive. This was for him a great work of God by the power of His Spirit. He could see that there might be some unfortunate descriptions of it, and was keenly aware of how some would take it, but he wanted to spread the news of God's work of revival far and wide.

Revival in Britain: Whitefield and the Wesleys

In Britain, the Evangelical Revival was first led by the Anglican minister George Whitefield. At a young age, he was used by God to bring the same conviction of the gospel that Edwards had seen in Northampton. Whitefield focused on the need for regeneration – being born again – feeling that the crucial issue in the church of his day was nominal religion that was missing this vital work of the Spirit.

What was so unusual about Whitefield, though, was not what he said – people like Watts had been emphasizing the need for regeneration for decades – but how he said it. Whitefield preached in the open air, rather than in churches, and this was extraordinary in his day. He also preached with great plainness and rhetoric which was certainly unusual in the Church of England, and was a step on from what was considered good taste within dissent.

The most unusual thing, of course, was what God chose to do through Whitefield. People came to hear him in the thousands – many coming to faith. This was dismissed by many as 'enthusiasm' once again, and Whitefield was regarded by many as an uncouth upstart and was banned from speaking in many churches. When Watts was asked for his assessment of Whitefield, one of his early comments was this:

> My opinion is that Whitefield does more good by his wild notes than we do with our set music.[12]

---

12   Fountain, *Watts*, p. 93.

Watts later met Whitefield a number of times. He had a variety of concerns, but his overall assessment remained very positive:

> I freely told him that I believed him to be a man of serious piety and uncommon zeal for the gospel of Christ, that God has blessed his labours and ministrations in the fields when he was shut out of the churches, and that in the main the gospel which he preached and his desire for the conversion of souls and the edification of Christians upon evangelical principles was the same as he would find in many of our dissenting churches if he could hear them ...[13]

One of the things Whitefield became known for was the extraordinary amount of preaching he did – many, many hours a day, day after day. Watts thought that this sheer amount of activity was itself a divine testimony that God was behind his ministry:

> I told him also that there was something that looked uncommon and extraordinary that a man of no strong constitution should be able to preach, expound, exhort and pray five or six hours in a day for many days together and not destroy his nature by it. So that his very continuance in life under such labours was the most divine, tangible evidence of an extraordinary call that I could find.[14]

Watts' summary was that all he could say to Whitefield was, 'Go on and prosper!'

However, there were aspects of Whitefield's ministry that Watts was concerned about. The main issue was what Watts called his 'imprudencies'. These were some of the great claims Whitefield occasionally made: for example, claims of how God was using him or prophecies about his ministry. Whitefield claimed a divine origin to these declarations. Watts' response was, 'How can we know that is true?' This was one of the classic issues of 'enthusiasm': people claiming that God had spoken to them, or given them a message. But unless there was some other corroboration, why should anyone else listen?

---

13   Watts, 'Letters,' p. 374.
14   Ibid., p. 375.

So, Watts reported on one of his conversations with Whitefield where he challenged him over these claims to divine 'impressions':

> He has acknowledged to me in conversation, that it is such an impression upon his own mind that he knows to be divine, though he cannot give me any convincing proof of it. I said many things to warn him of the dangers of delusion, and to guard him against the irregularities and imprudences which youth and zeal might lead him into, and told him plainly, that though I believed him very sincere and desirous to do good to souls, yet I was not convinced of any extraordinary call he had to some parts of his conduct; and he seemed to take this free discourse in a very candid and modest manner.[15]

Whitefield also made some damning statements about the Church of England, such as that a previous Archbishop 'knew no more of Christianity than Mohammed'. Watts cringed at such statements, probably partly because he was a much more moderate character, but also because they were over the top! Whitefield himself hadn't meant some of these statements to become public, but overly zealous friends had published some of his personal writing on his behalf. Watts said:

> I cannot but say I have a great love for the man, and he seems to have been raised up like Luther in the Reformation from Popery, to rouse the generality of the Church of England from its formalities in religion and from some of the growing errors of the times; but I fear he has done himself and his ministry unspeakable hurt by these letters which are now published... I pray God keep good Mr Whitefield from any more such imprudencies...[16]

The tension between the older, cautious Watts and the younger, exuberant Whitefield remained. Watts continued to lament signs of 'enthusiasm' and 'imprudencies', but still spoke of God's great work through Whitefield. One of his last comments on Whitefield is:

---

15 Milner, *Watts*, p. 638.
16 Watts, 'Letters,' p. 379.

My converse with him is not much, nor am I esteemed one of his admirers; but I own myself to admire the grace of God in him and the power of God that supports him.[17]

Watts, then, was positive about Whitefield, but with reservations.

Watts was less sure about John and Charles Wesley. There was not as much contact between him and them, and consequently we have little to go on. Watts does reveal, however, that he feels the Wesleys weren't securely doctrinally anchored. He refers to their different sentiments as being against certain Calvinistic doctrines (which emphasize God's sovereignty in salvation) such as election and the perseverance of the saints. Watts was a moderate Calvinist himself and was quite cautious over some standard Calvinistic positions; but Calvinist he was still and in his day such distinctions made a lot of difference.

He was also concerned about the Wesleys' focus on feelings in conversion. As we've seen, Watts was no enemy of emotion; quite the opposite, he encouraged it. But he was against anyone specifying what you had to feel, or insisting on the necessity of certain feelings. So he speaks of his concerns about the Wesleys 'in preaching up the necessity of conscious feelings of our regeneration'.[18] His final concern was their doctrine of 'Christian perfection', which involved Christians attaining a state where they do not consciously sin.

He did meet John and Charles at one point, but we have no comment made on that meeting from Watts. John Wesley records the meeting in his journal:

Wednesday 4 Oct. 1738

1.30 at Dr. Watts', conversed; 2.30 walked, singing, conversed...[19]

---

17 Ibid., p. 402.

18 Ibid., p. 375.

19 John Wesley, *Journal of Rev. John Wesley*, ed. N. Curnock (London, 1928), Volume 2, p. 82.

This time of conversation and singing included Charles Wesley as well, and so the two greatest hymn writers in the English language sang together.

The Wesleys had great respect for Watts and especially for his hymns, which they made constant use of. In the first hymn book John Wesley compiled, one-third of the hymns were from Watts.

Watts, no doubt, would have said that God was using the Wesleys in the revival and honoured them for that. But his concerns would have remained.

Summary

Watts had longed for the days of revival. Many of his works speak of his pain over the church of his day, lamenting that 'the glory of God has much departed'. All this meant he rejoiced to see revival come.

However, his was not pure joy. He saw errors and dangers within the revival. He was much more positive about the work in New England than in England itself. It is possible that this is because in New England the revival was linked with nonconformist churches, whereas in England it came through the Anglican Church. But this is only speculation: nothing Watts said supports that argument.

He was also more positive about the ministry of Whitefield than that of the Wesleys. Even with Whitefield he had significant concerns. But within the reservations he continued to say that God was at work and there was reason to rejoice.

This mixed reaction is seen in a preface Watts was asked to write for a book which described the revival in New England and was published in London in 1744. Watts wrote the preface to recommend it as the best account of the revival so far.[20] He spends his preface defending the revival while admitting that some parts of it are wrong.

For instance, he says:

---

20 Congregational Churches in Massachusetts, *The testimony and advice of an assembly of pastors of churches in New England, at a meeting in Boston, July 7, 1743. With a recommendation of it by the Revd. Dr. Watts.* (London: J. Oswald, 1744).

The evidences of this work, so far as they are durable and lasting, seem to me to be very conformable to Scripture, and carry in them sufficient reason to raise and support our belief.

However, he quickly goes on:

It is granted... that there have been several great errors arising there; particularly antinomian and enthusiastic opinions have broken forth amongst them, and some disorderly practices appeared, such as young preachers and exhorters wandering through their towns without any apparent and regular call of any kind either from God or men.

Watts points to the possible sources of such errors:

... they all evidently arise from the mixed state of things in this world, from the follies and imperfections of even good Christians, from the weakness and real madness of some men, together with the wickedness of others, and perhaps also from the malice of fallen angels [devils] endeavouring to darken and disgrace the work of the Spirit of God on the soul.

He goes on to say that the people who have written in this book have seen and acknowledged these errors but still cannot deny the evidence of a real work of God. His conclusion is that while 'irregularities' clearly exist, they do not mean God is not at work:

So far as I can judge these are by no means sufficient to destroy the evidence that the work is divine. And I hope that in due time the rays of the sun of righteousness will scatter all these mists which obscure his glorious work, and that the power of Christ in the conversion of souls shall appear illustrious, and be honoured according to its merit.

Watts saw the revival as a work of God but one that contained errors and irregularities. And he would say that such errors were more obvious in some areas and ministries than in others. But that was to be expected, and the real grace of God at work was not to be denied. In the last analysis, he rejoiced that he had lived to see revival.

11

LIFE DRAWING TO A CLOSE

The last period of Watts' life continued in very much the same manner as we have seen already. He continued to live with the Abney family, enjoying their support and hospitality. He continued as pastor but with frequent periods of illness such that he was unable to preach or visit his congregation. He also continued to write and, in fact, was remarkably productive over the last decade of his life.

The World to Come

One of his later works that is worth commenting on, published in 1739 (with a second part in 1745), is about the future. It is called:

> The World to Come; or, Discourses on the Joys or Sorrows of Departed Souls at Death, and the Glory or Terror of the Resurrection.

Watts had written on this topic before, but this was him at his best. One cannot help but think that much of the content was written in the great awareness and expectation of his own impending death. Some parts of it had been written earlier on occasions of bereavement. It is, therefore, written in the certain knowledge that we will die. Such a perspective is relatively rare to find today, and there is much we can learn from Watts on this.

Within this work, a sermon entitled 'The End of Time' was also published separately as a tract. It was very popular and was translated into many other languages. It is a meditation on the simple idea that time as we know it here and now will one day end. Watts says:[1]

> Eternity comes upon us at once, and all that we enjoy, all that we do, and all that we suffer in time, shall be no longer.

Watts proceeds to make a series of simple but profound observations. The reality of death means that the opportunity for responding to the gospel will one day end: 'this life is the only time given to us for this important change'. Contrary to some Christian writers today, Watts sees that there is no opportunity for salvation beyond death:

> The sound of God's mercy reaches not to the realms of the dead; those who die before they are reconciled, they die under the load of all their sins and must perish for ever, without the least hope or glimpse of reconciling or forgiving grace.

This leads Watts to plead with people to make sure they have responded to the gospel before it is too late: 'Have I such an interest in the covenant as takes away the sting of death, as turns the curse into a blessing, and changes the dark scenes of death into the commencement of a new and everlasting life?'

Watts goes on to speak of the end of all the physical things around us which can bring happiness and delight in this life. Since they will one day end, he advises: 'Have a care then that you do not make any of them your chief hope, for they are but the things of time, they are all short and dying enjoyments.'

He observes what a terrible and awful day the day of judgment will be for those who do not trust in Christ. But rather than simply state this, Watts helps his readers feel it:

---

1   All the following references to this work are in Watts, *Works*, 'The World to Come', Volume 1.

Who knows how keen and bitter will be the agonies of an awakened conscience and the vengeance of a provoked God in that world of misery? How will you cry out, 'O what a wretch I have been, to renounce all the advices of a compassionate Father, when he would have persuaded me to improve the time of youth and health. Alas, I turned a deaf ear to his advice, and now time is lost and my hopes of mercy for ever perished...'

He finishes with some reflections:

- How valuable time is: 'every hour you live is an hour longer given to you to prepare for dying, and to save a soul.'

- We should be aware of the advance of time and the arrival of the end. Each new day, birthday, new year or bereavement, should make us think: 'Take this warning, O my soul, and think of thine own removal!'

- What stupidity it is to be aware of the coming end and yet to waste the time given to us, looking for ways to 'kill time': 'O that these loiterers would once consider, that time loiters not!'

- Learn that God is merciful in warning us that time will end and in giving us time to respond: 'Every day and every hour is a mercy of unknown importance to sinful men.'

- How useful it is to picture ourselves at the end of time: 'imagine ourselves ... at the tribunal of Christ and to call our souls to a solemn account.'

- Learn the wonderful happiness of those who have used the time they have been given well and look forward to Jesus' return: 'Happy souls indeed, who have so valued time, as not to let it run off in trifles, but have obtained treasures more valuable than that time which is gone, even the riches of the covenant of grace, and the hopes of an eternal inheritance in glory.' The time of struggle, pain and battle is over; joy and delight has come.

Watts ends with this thought for the Christian:

> The stream of time, which has run between the banks of this mortal life, and bore you along amidst many dangerous rocks of temptation, fear, and sorrow, shall launch you out into the ocean of pleasures, which have no limit, those felicities must be everlasting, for duration has no limit there. Time with all its measures, shall be no more.

This is Watts at his rhetorical best taking a Biblical doctrine, holding it up to light to be seen clearly, and then impressing it on the heart to be felt deeply.

Other works

A number of other publications came in the last decade of Watts' life, including some we've looked at already. His wide range of writing is shown again by the fact that one of his works was on the separation of religious and civil power. In his childhood, of course, Watts had known the results of civil authorities taking religious matters into their own hands – this is what resulted in 'dissent' from the national church and the imprisonment of Watts' father. Through the rest of his life, Watts had known the toleration of dissent, but not the equality of it, again because of the civil power intruding into religion.

In light of these events, Watts' work *A New Essay on Civil Power in Things Sacred* (1739) argued for freedom of religion according to each person's conscience. Watts argued that the state should restrict itself to enforcement of general morality, not religious practice. His was one of a growing number of voices arguing for such freedom and separation of church and state.

A few years later, Watts wrote *The Harmony of all the Religions which God ever Prescribed* (1742). This was a survey through the Bible of the different ways God has related to mankind. Watts' aim was once again to show the reasonableness of the Christian faith, this time by demonstrating the consistency of the Bible. Watts said this book was:

> ... a compendious arrangement of the discoveries of the
> grace of God and the duty of man, in such an order as
> God has prescribed them, and such as may best show their
> consistency their reasonableness and equity.[2]

Watts argued that since the Fall God has acted towards
people with great consistency: He has always asked for
faith in His covenant promise. This put the lie to the
idea that in the Old Testament people were saved by their
works and in the New Testament people were saved by
their faith, or that the Old Testament was plan A, and the
New Testament was plan B – ideas that unfortunately still
circulate today.

Watts also addressed one of the ongoing debates of the
day which we considered in earlier chapters. Some people
emphasized that all God asked for was faith – so much so,
in fact, that they went on to say it didn't really matter how
a Christian lived. This position was called 'antinomianism'
(being against the law). However, others emphasized that
Christians had to live obeying God. This could drift into
legalism where you looked to your obedience to save you.
Getting a right orientation of being saved by faith alone,
but then living to please God, has often been difficult in
church history. The world of dissent in the eighteenth
century was a time when it was particularly difficult, with
different groups falling out with each other over the issue.

Watts was careful to show how faith always resulted in
a change in life throughout the Bible:

> Let it always be remembered, as under all former
> dispensations, so under the Christian, that this faith can
> never justify us if it be a dead faith, that is, such a faith as
> produces no good works, that is, where there is time and
> opportunity for them.

The last phrase here about time and opportunity is
important. Watts wanted to say that someone who had
true faith was saved, even if there was then no chance to
live differently. Our obedient life does not save us – it is all

---

2   All the following references are from ibid., 'Harmony', Volume 2.

by faith – but true faith will show itself in life. Watts also pointed out very clearly that faith is faith, not a type of work. It is, in fact, the opposite of any work:

> But faith or trust is that act of the soul, whereby we renounce our own works as the ground of our justification or acceptance; we acknowledge our own imperfection, unworthiness and insufficiency, and give the entire honour to divine grace, by our dependence on it. We are saved by grace, that God may have the glory of all.

Watts published a number of other works in the last few years of life. These were mainly writings from earlier years which he simply had to prepare for the press, as his health was now quite poor. One of these was *Orthodoxy and Charity United* (1745). This was Watts' attempt to get different groups of believers in his day to agree with each other, especially those involved in the recent revivals and the old guard. He always hated disunity and suggested here, perhaps slightly naively, that it often stemmed from misunderstandings.

He argued for the central truths of the gospel which all must be united on; here he again argued against the deists and others who had lost central parts of the gospel. But, he said, there are many secondary areas in which we should grant liberty to other Christians who see things differently. Watts discusses these disputed areas and gives his own opinion on them; but his main aim is to show that they should not be a cause for disunity. In many ways, Watts was ahead of his time in this. In his day, people fell out over what we would regard as minor points of doctrine, and Watts was calling for a more charitable position.

This call for unity was characteristic of Watts as a personality. Dr Johnson said of him: 'It was not only in his book, but in his mind also, that orthodoxy and charity were united.'[3]

There were brand new works Watts wanted to write, but he decided he did not have the health and energy to do

---

3   Milner, *Watts*, p. 675.

so. One of these was a book that examined the progress of God's work in people, beginning with their understanding of the gospel and going on to their growth in grace. Rather than writing it himself, he entrusted the project to Philip Doddridge. Watts had outlined the scheme of the book but left it to Doddridge to actually write it. It was called *The Rise and Progress of Religion in the Soul.*

Doddridge pressed on, knowing that Watts' health was poor. He wrote in 1743, 'I am hard at work on my book of the 'Rise and Progress of Religion', which Dr Watts is impatient to see, and I am eager to finish, lest he should slip away to heaven before it is done.'

Watts wrote to Doddridge in 1744:

> I long to have your 'Rise and Progress' appear in the world. I wish my health had been so far established, that I could have read over every line with the attention it merits; but I am not ashamed by what I have read, to recommend it as the best treatise on practical religion which is to be found in our language, and I pray God that it may be extensively beneficial.[4]

Watts gave advice on what Doddridge had written. He had envisioned a book which could be read by anyone, and so he tried it out on some of the servants of the house. This led him to encourage Doddridge to 'reduce the language into easier words and plainer periods.'

The book was finally published in 1745. Doddridge dedicated it to Watts:

> With the most affectionate gratitude and respect, I beg leave to present you a book, which owes its existence to your request, its copiousness to your plan, and much of its perspicuity to your review, and to the use I made of your remarks on that part of it which your health and leisure would permit you to examine.

This became an extremely popular book and was translated into many different languages – presumably achieving some of the benefit Watts had prayed for.

---

4   Ibid., p. 628.

Increasing weakness and troubles

In the 1740s, Watts' always intermittent health was gradually going downhill. His letters over the last few years of his life often speak of being confined to bed or enduring various 'nervous disorders'. In particular, he suffered from insomnia. As was standard in his day, he took medication for this in the form of opiate drugs. The effect of these soon wore off, however, and his sleeplessness became worse.

His health was still up and down, though. In 1743, he wrote to Doddridge:

> I thank God I am so far recovered from that severe and dangerous illness, which seized me a fortnight ago, that I can sit in my chamber and dictate this letter. If God raise me up to any usefulness I am cheerfully ready; if not, I cheerfully resign every thing that is mortal at his order.[5]

He was, as he put in his letters, on 'the borders of life'. He had written of death as sleep and the desirability of it in his book *The World to Come*:

> Why, O my fearful soul, should thou be afraid of dying? Why should thou be frightened at the dark shadows of the grave, when thou art weary with the toils and crosses of the day? Hast thou not often desired the shadow of the evening and longed for the bed of natural sleep, where thy fatigues and thy sorrows may be forgotten for a season? And is not the grave itself a sweet sleeping place for the saints, wherein they lie down and forget their distresses, and feel one of the miseries of human life, and especially since it is softened and sanctified by the Son of God lying down there? Why should thou be afraid to lay thy head in the dust? It is but entering into God's hiding place, into his chambers of rest and repose.

There was a painful personal episode involving his nephew, James Brackstone, in 1746. We don't know the details, but Doddridge wrote to his wife about it, saying:

> His nephew, once so great a favourite, has done something to vex him, and his poor weak spirits cannot bear it; so

---

5   Ibid., p. 629.

that he is quite amazed, and even stupefied with it to such a degree as hardly to take notice of anything else about him...[6]

Someone else wrote to Doddridge about the same event the following year:

> The behaviour of Dr Richard Watts and the wretch Brackstone towards Dr Watts is a most marvellous, infamous, enormous wickedness.

It seems that Lady Abney kept some of the worst details back from Watts himself for fear of their effect. However, he clearly knew enough as he wrote to his friend Benjamin Colman in Boston:

> As for my nephew, James Brackstone, I would have you for the future neither send nor write any thing to him relating to me. He has dealt so wickedly and shamefully with me that our church has cast him out a great while ago and I have done with him entirely...

Last days

In 1747, when asked how he was, he was known to reply, 'Waiting God's leave to die'. He sometimes agonized over that waiting, though:

> Sometimes I have been ready to say within myself, 'Why is my life prolonged in sorrow? Why are my days lengthened out to see further wretchedness? Methinks that grace should be ready for me and the house appointed for all the living. What further can I do for God or for men here on earth, since my nature pines away with wasteful sickness, my nerves are unstrung, my spirits dissipated, and my best powers of acting are enfeebled and almost lost? Peace, peace, O thou complaining spirit. Dost thou know the counsels of the Almighty, and the secret designs of thy God and thy Saviour? He had many deep and unknown purposes in continuing his children amidst heavy sorrows, which they can never penetrate or learn in this world. Silence and submission become thee at all times.'

---

6   Davis, *Watts*, p. 64.

As mentioned in an earlier chapter, there are various reports of Watts losing lucidity and becoming deranged in his last days. However, the reports of those closest to him contain no such elements. Certainly he seems to have been clear in his ongoing trust in Christ.

A minister had once said to Watts that when the most knowledgeable and learned Christians came to die, they only had the same plain promises of the gospel to trust in as everyone else. Watts relayed this to a friend and added:

> And so I find it. They are the plain promises of the gospel which are my support, and I bless God they are plain promises, which do not require much labour or pains to understand them, for I can do nothing now but look into my Bible for some promise to support me and live on that.[7]

His assistant noted down some of his last statements. One of these was:

> It is a great mercy to me that I have no manner of fear or dread of death. I could, if God please, lay my head back and die without terror this afternoon or night. My chief supports are from my view of eternal things and the interest I have in them. I trust all my sins are pardoned through the blood of Christ. I have no fear of dying; it would be my greatest comfort to lie down and sleep and wake no more.[8]

Finally on 25 November 1748, Watts died. He was seventy-four years old.

Watts had given directions for his funeral. The service was carried out by two Independent ministers, two Presbyterian and two Baptist. He was buried, at his request, in Bunhill Fields. This was a cemetery used by dissenters, and many famous Puritans, such as John Owen and John Bunyan, are buried there.

Watts had composed his own epitaph:

> Isaac Watts, D.D. pastor of a church of Christ in London, successor to the Rev. Mr. Joseph Caryl, Dr. John Owen,

---

7   Hood, *Watts*, p. 262.

8   Milner, *Watts*, p. 698.

Mr. David Clarkson, and Dr. Isaac Chauncy, after fifty years of feeble labours in the gospel, interrupted by four years of tiresome sickness, was at last dismissed to his rest – Nov. 25, A.D. 1748, age 75.

"In Uno Jesus Omnia."

2 Cor. 5,8. 'Absent from the body, present with the Lord.'

Col. 3,4. 'When Christ who is our life shall appear, I shall also appear with Him in Glory.'

The funeral sermon was preached by his friend Dr David Jennings, his assistant Samuel Price not feeling up to the task. He spoke from Hebrews 11:4, 'By it, he being dead, yet speaketh'. Jennings explained that Watts, like Abel in the passage, was still speaking through his example and his writings. He went on:

> While he is now celebrating the new songs of heaven, how many thousands of pious worshippers are this day lifting up their hearts to God in the sacred songs he taught them upon earth! Though his 'voice' is not any longer heard by us, yet his 'words', like those of the day and the night, are 'gone out to the end of the world'.[9]

There were many eulogies in the press, many sermons preached and a number of poems written on the occasion of Watts' death. The following is a concise but representative example from *The Gentleman's Magazine*:

> Isaac Watts, a truly ingenious and accomplished person as well in polite literature as in Divinity and the Sciences of which his writings as well poetical as prosaic abundantly testify, and no less exemplary for candour, piety, and solid virtue. He was a Dissenting Minister but honoured by all parties.

Various statues have been erected in significant places. There is one in Abney Park in Stoke Newington which was created from part of the grounds of the Abney family

---

9   David Jennings, *Funeral Sermon for the Late Reverend Isaac Watts* (London: Oswald and Dilly, 1749), p. 3.

estate. Another is in Southampton in Watts Park. There is also a bust of him in Westminster Abbey.

Conclusion

Isaac Watts is known today as a hymn writer, and it must be said it was in his hymns that he has the claim to genius. People vary as to whom they think was the best hymn writer of all time, but it usually comes down to a choice between Charles Wesley and Isaac Watts. Watts is often said to win, if only on the basis that he came first and Wesley could use him as a starting point.

But there was so much more to Watts than his hymns. Others have written far more, but his literary output was still extensive. Others have produced more original works, but his were still insightful and helpful. Others have defended the faith against greater threat, but he still fought significant fights in his day.

Perhaps one of the most impressive things to see is the vast range of his writing. He wrote for children and for adults; he explained theology and natural science; he debated with philosophers and penned songs for four-year-olds; he produced textbooks which were used at universities and he wrote pastoral letters for hurting people in his congregation.

He was also very balanced. At a time when reason was being exalted, he happily agreed with the advances in science and logic, but still pointed out the shortcomings of our reasoning and the need for revelation. At a time when churches were firmly divided into different parties, he argued for the central doctrines of the faith which we must unite on, but for tolerance in secondary matters. At a time when religion was becoming dry and rational, he argued fervently for the need for heart religion, but still warned about the need for clear thinking. At a time when revival struck, he welcomed it and rejoiced in it but still warned of some of the excesses he saw.

At its worst, that sense of balance could lead to taking a middle-of-the-road position on everything; that accusation is sometimes made of Watts, and not unreasonably. However, it is only half true. His instinct was for a compromise position, but not because he simply wanted to please both sides. Rather, he appreciated different sides to an argument. Also, he didn't simply choose any middle position; rather, the particular position he took was carefully thought over and argued for.

One reader commented to Watts about why he appreciated his writing so much:

> What gives me a particular relish for your books is that, with the strongest sentiments of piety to God, there is always joined the most extensive charity to men, and a happy freedom from the bigotry of party opinions.[10]

This comment moves us to see the link between Watts' writing and his character. Watts' aim was to serve the church. He wanted his writing to be useful, and this shaped both what and how he wrote. He did write with charity to others but also with a clear conscience before God.

Above his writing we should see the man and the Christian. One of the aspects of Watts which was highlighted after his death was his character. In his funeral sermon, David Jennings specifically focused on his humility:

> His humility was like a deep shade, if I may so express it, that set off his other graces and virtues, and made them shine with a brighter lustre. And as this grace had a mighty influence on his heart and temper, so it had no little effect in forming his sentiments. For he never thought he could be laid too low, as a Creature or a Sinner, that he might do honour to the perfections and grace of God... Nor was his humility less conspicuous in his outward carriage and behaviour towards others. From hence flowed that condescension and gentleness, that humanity and kindness, that could not but endear him to all who had the pleasure of conversing with him; and which rendered him truly venerable, in a much higher degree, than all the honours and applauses, he received from the world.[11]

---

10   Gibbons, *Memoirs*, p. 441.

11   Jennings, *Funeral Sermon for the Late Reverend Isaac Watts*, pp. 29-30.

Watts composed some lines which are presumed to have been written to go alongside his portrait. They are certainly suitable for that, and suitable too to summarize his identity as a minister of Christ, but most fundamentally as a man in Christ:

> In Christ my life is safe reposed,
> I glory in his name;
> Him, whom my tongue and pen disclosed,
> My portrait shall proclaim.
> Jesus! My whole felicity
> Is centred and comprised in thee.

Also available from Christian Focus ...

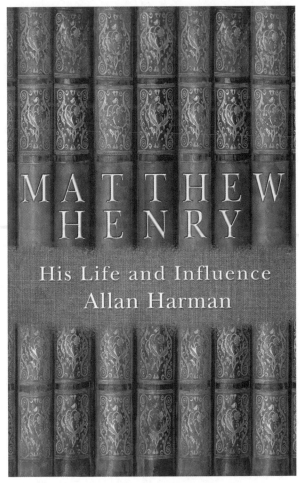

MATTHEW HENRY

His Life and Influence
Allan Harman

ISBN 978-1-84550-783-1

Matthew Henry

His Life and Influence

ALLAN HARMAN

Matthew Henry (1662-1714) is highly-valued by contemporary preachers and Bible users. Here we get a closer look at the life of Matthew Henry by an author who has had a life-long interest in Matthew Henry and his writings. Matthew Henry was the son of a Puritan pastor who had been silenced by the government of the time. Nevertheless Philip Henry, a godly man reared his family on Christian principles and Matthew followed the Lord from an early age. Although it was difficult to find suitable ministerial training, Matthew Henry eventually studied for the ministry. With government opposition relaxing, he became a Presbyterian pastor in Chester in 1687 and later in London from 1712. It is astonishing to note the amount of preaching and writing that he accomplished despite suffering from ill-health and knowing intense sorrow in his family life.

Allan Harman has had a life-time interest in exposition of the biblical text, and also in the history of interpretation. He is Research Professor of Old Testament at the Presbyterian Theological College in Melbourne, Australia. He has lectured and preached in many countries, and continues to serve as the senior editor of the Reformed Theological Review, Australia's oldest theological journal.

"This book is a celebration of God's grace..." **John Stott**

GENIUS, GRIEF & GRACE
A Doctor Looks at Suffering & Success
DR. GAIUS DAVIES

CASE STUDIES:
Martin Luther, John Bunyan, William Cowper, Lord Shaftesbury,
Christina Rossetti, Frances R. Havergal, Gerard Manley Hopkins,
Amy Carmichael, C.S. Lewis, J.B. Philips, Martyn Lloyd-Jones.

ISBN 978-1-84550-359-8

Genius, Grief & Grace
A Doctor Looks at Suffering and Success
Gaius Davies

Dr. Gaius Davies introduces us to Martin Luther, John Bunyan, William Cowper, Lord Shaftesbury, Gerard Manly Hopkins, Christina Rossetti, Amy Carmichael, J.B. Phillips, C.S. Lewis, Martyn Lloyd-Jones and Frances Ridley Havergal.

After a brief biographical introduction to each person, he shows us how he or she all had their particular trial, and how grace operated in each of them.

He is not afraid to show how anxiety, guilt, depression and doubt can be present in the finest of Christian lives, but also goes on to show how divine grace can transform human weakness.

Dr. Gaius Davies, FRCPsych, M Phil, DPM, was a Consultant Psychiatrist at King's College Hospital, London. He is a well-respected author.

John
∴CALVIN∷

HIS LIFE & INFLUENCE

∴

∷ROBERT L. REYMOND∷

ISBN 978-1-85792-966-9

John Calvin

His Life and Influence

ROBERT L. REYMOND

'...despite his stern Calvinist upbringing' – Why is it that in the modern media the word 'Calvinist' is always accompanied by 'stern', 'dour' or 'strict'? Most of the people who use the terms together have next to no knowledge of what Calvinism is - and know even less about who Calvin was. An old-style reactionary? A hard-line ayatollah, raging at the world without any thought? - or is there more to this man than uninformed contemporary critics would have us believe?

Robert Reymond brings us John Calvin the man. A reality quite different from the caricature often painted today. Here is a man of deep spirituality with a real love for his fellow man and God. A man also with tremendous intellectual abilities. Whether the moniker 'stern Calvinist' is applicable or not - his life has much to teach us.

Robert L. Reymond taught for more than 25 years on the faculties of Covenant Theological Seminary (St. Louis, Missouri) and Knox Theological Seminary (Ft. Lauderdale, Florida). He holds a B.A., M.A., and Ph.D. degrees from Bob Jones University and did post-doctoral studies at Fuller Seminary, New York University, Union Seminary (New York), Tyndale House, Cambridge, and Rutherford House, Edinburgh.

THE LIFE, BOOKS & INFLUENCE OF
—— JOHN BUNYAN ——

GRACE
ABOUNDING

DAVID CALHOUN

ISBN 978-1-84550-031-3

Grace Abounding

The Life, Books and Influence of John Bunyan

DAVID CALHOUN

The Pilgrim's Progress written by John Bunyan is one of the most famous and well-read books of the English language.

David Calhoun tells us about Bunyan's life as well as analysing his books and theology. Bunyan was an English Baptist pastor whose influence through 'The Pilgrim's Progress' could be said to have shaped the British and American psyche. Bunyan was more than an imprisoned tinker with time on his hands, he wrote many other books and was a key figure in British history during momentous nation- changing events.David includes summaries of Pilgrim's Progress (parts 1 & 2), the Holy War, the Life and Death of Mr Badman (Bunyan's alternative to The Life and Death of Christian) and Bunyan's other writings. Useful appendices are included on contemporary places to visit on the trail of Bunyan and how Pilgrims Progress has been adapted for children.

David Calhoun has brought together a beautiful book on the life, works and influence of a famous historical figure. David B. Calhoun is Professor of Church History at Covenant Theological Seminary, St. Louis, Missouri. He studied with Francis Schaeffer and has led international ministry organizations in America and Europe. Among his writing credits is the definitive 2 volume history of Princeton Seminary.

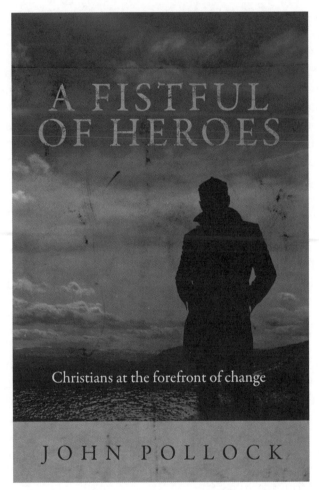

A FISTFUL
OF HEROES

Christians at the forefront of change

J O H N   P O L L O C K

ISBN 978-1-78191-204-1

A Fistful of Heroes
Christians at the forefront of Change
JOHN POLLOCK

We shouldn't be surprised when we have the examples in the Bible of David and Saul of Tarsus! John Pollock's deft, biographical pen sweeps over great reformers, liberators and evangelists of the 18th and 19th centuries. He shows their spiritual development, often from unpromising beginnings, and encourages us to believe that God can use us too. Characters include:

John Newton, William Wilberforce,
James Ramsey, Sir Charles Middleton,
Sir George Williams, The 7th Earl of Shaftsbury,
Robert Raikes, Elizabeth Fry,
Thomas 'Stonewall' Jackson, Sir Henry Havelock,
Sir Herbert Edwardes, D. L. Moody,
Brownlow North, R. A. Torrey,
Bramwell Booth, Lord Radstock
Hudson Taylor, Adoniram Judson,
Mildred Cable, Stanley Smith,
Rosalie Harvey, James Chalmers, Ernest Presswood,
John & Betty Stam, Sir Wilfred Grenfell,
Mary Slessor and Rowland Bingham

The late John Pollock, an award-winning biographer, had a flair for telling a dramatic story. He used this talent to write many biographies including ones on D. L. Moody and Major General Sir Henry Havelock.

Christian Focus Publications

Our mission statement –

STAYING FAITHFUL
In dependence upon God we seek to impact the world
through literature faithful to His infallible Word, the
Bible. Our aim is to ensure that the Lord Jesus Christ
is presented as the only hope to obtain forgiveness of
sin, live a useful life and look forward to heaven with
Him.

Our Books are published in four imprints:

CHRISTIAN
FOCUS

popular works including biographies, commentaries, basic
doctrine and Christian living.

CHRISTIAN
HERITAGE

books representing some of
the best material from the
rich heritage of the church.

MENTOR

books written at a level suitable for Bible College and
seminary students, pastors,
and other serious readers.
The imprint includes com-
mentaries, doctrinal studies, examination of current
issues and church history.

CF4•K

children's books for quality
Bible teaching and for all age
groups: Sunday school curriculum, puzzle and activity
books; personal and family
devotional titles, biographies
and inspirational stories –
Because you are never too
young to know Jesus!

Christian Focus Publications Ltd,
Geanies House, Fearn, Ross-shire,
IV20 1TW, Scotland, United Kingdom.
www.christianfocus.com